# Play Therapy

## Engaging & Powerful Techniques for the Treatment of Childhood Disorders

ADHD-Anxiety-Autism-Disruptive Behavior Disorders-

Depression-OCD-Self-Esteem-Social Skills-Trauma-PTSD

## Clair Mellenthin, LCSW, RPT-S

*Play Therapy: Engaging & Powerful Techniques for the Treatment of Childhood Disorders*
Copyright © 2018 Clair Mellenthin, LCSW, RPT-S

Published by
PESI Publishing & Media
PESI, Inc.
3839 White Ave
Eau Claire, WI 54703

Cover Design: Amy Rubenzer
Layout: Bookmasters & Amy Rubenzer
Editing: Bookmasters

Proudly printed in the United States of America

ISBN: 9781683731122

# About the Author

**Clair Mellenthin**, **LCSW, RPT-S**, holds a Master's Degree in Social Work from the University of Southern California. Throughout her career, she has focused on providing play therapy to children, teens, and their families. She is currently the Director of Child and Adolescents at Wasatch Family Therapy. Ms. Mellenthin is a sought-after supervisor, training graduate students and interns in play therapy, and an adjunct faculty member at the University of Southern California as part of the MSW program. She is the past president of the Utah Association for Play Therapy and remains an active member on the Board of Directors. She is also the author of *My Many Colors of Me Workbook*. In addition to being an experienced play therapist and professor, Ms. Mellenthin frequently presents professional play therapy and family therapy trainings and appears on local and national TV and radio as an expert on child and family issues.

# Acknowledgements

This book would not be complete without the many contributions of my fellow play therapy colleagues and friends. I am beyond grateful for Dr. Robert Jason Grant, who was willing to share his time and expertise in treating Autism Spectrum Disorder (ASD) utilizing play therapy. Dr. Grant has created AutPlay, which is a phenomenal certification program in the treatment of ASD utilizing the powers of play therapy. A special thank you to Shirla Pamp, LMFT, RPT; Melanie Davis, LCMHC, NCC; and John Burr, LCSW, RPT-S, for their expressive arts contributions. Tammi Van Hollander, LCSW, RPT, shared her empowering sand tray intervention, and Dr. Gary York, PhD, RPT, shared his creative games for social skills. This list wouldn't be complete without thanking my friend and colleague Holly Willard, LCSW, RPT-S, for sharing her play therapy interventions to treat trauma. I am a better therapist because of each of these amazing clinicians and am grateful to call them my friends. A special thank you to Dr. Risë VanFleet for writing the forward to this book and being a mentor, supporter, and friend.

I also need to thank my editor, Karsyn Morse, who always made herself available to answer my many questions, review content, and show support and excitement for this book to blossom. Thank you to my Wasatch Family Therapy family and friends for being excited and so supportive of this book.

This book would never have happened without the support and love from my husband Matt and my sweet children, Matt, Marissa, and Sami whose beautiful faces grace these pages. They have been the world's best teachers on how to be a better mom, wife, therapist, and friend.

# Table of Contents

# Foreword

"Play is the highest form of research." The brilliant physicist Albert Einstein wrote a great deal about play and imagination, and he held both in high regard. When asked which he trusted more, knowledge or imagination, he said, "Imagination is more important than knowledge. Knowledge is limited. Imagination encircles the world." Nowadays when so much emphasis is placed on children's acquisition of knowledge, these words and concepts need to be revisited. When schools reduce or eliminate recess and extracurricular activities in pursuit of higher test scores, the results might ultimately be disappointing. Play and imagination are critical for child development and learning as well as for society's development, and their role in furthering knowledge and opening new ideas and opportunities should not be underestimated.

Children use play and imagination to explore the world and to make sense of what they see, hear, and experience. Play strengthens the connections in the brain and supports intellectual, physical, emotional, social, and creative processes. It fosters problem-solving and builds social relationships. The process of healthy attachment involves the creation of a secure base, usually with parents, from which the child can explore the wider world while knowing they have a safe relationship to which they can periodically retreat. When emotional events occur in children's lives, their primary method for understanding them is to play about them.

As I watched the unfolding of the horrible and massive floods in Houston, I was reminded of my many years being involved in disaster mental health in one role or another. Regardless of country or type of traumatic event, when children have the opportunity, they play out what they have seen as they try to understand what it means for them. They do this naturally as long as they are permitted to. In my clinical work, I have seen this as well. When children are struggling with car accidents, parental discord and divorce, separation, bereavement, medical conditions, abuse, violence, school pressures, bullying, and other challenges, they play in ways that help them understand and cope. Some of this play can be repetitive with minor changes to the storyline that suggests the gradual mastery of the scary feelings—fear, anxiety, sadness, anger, helplessness, and others—that accompany the event or situation. It's what children do all the time, if we stop and simply watch what they are doing.

Play therapy harnesses this natural inclination to play to create emotionally-safe therapeutic environments that foster communication, relationship-building, expression, problem-resolution, and mastery. The past 30 years have seen the field grow rapidly while research supports the use of play therapy to help resolve many different types of child and family problems. Play therapy is theoretically-grounded, empirically-supported, and most importantly, focused on the unique strengths and needs of each child and his or her family. The methods are many, but these three factors distinguish it from "just playing with kids." It is a discipline for which one must train, be supervised, and gain experience. On the surface, using play to assist children sounds simple enough, but it is a far more complex endeavor.

Each child and family that seeks assistance is unique, so therapists must adapt what they do to recognize and honor that uniqueness. This requires a solid background in mental health treatment as well as great skill in applying the many options offered by the field of play therapy to one unique situation after another. One never stops learning. The responses of children and their families to play-based interventions is often remarkable and gratifying. Resources have been increasing rapidly through recent decades, and therapists not only have access to many expressive and play therapy techniques, but they also have a greater community of like-minded therapists with whom to share ideas.

Children live in a context, that of family. Their parents, siblings, and extended families have great influence. This can be the source of some of their problems, but it can also be a big part of the solutions. Relationships are built on two-way streets, so helping parents change can be critical to supporting the interventions a therapist conducts with a child. Furthermore, parents can be integrated into treatment in ways that help the whole family make changes together. For these reasons, I have always championed play therapy approaches that make room for parents and families to be involved one way or another.

In her book, *Play Therapy: Engaging & Powerful Techniques for the Treatment of Childhood Disorders*, Clair Mellenthin offers play therapy ideas and interventions without forgetting about the theoretical foundations and the family. In this well-written volume, she discusses the importance of play and the value of an attachment theory focus when intervening with families. She couples the "how" to intervene with the "why." She has organized the chapters by problem area, and then for each, she and her guest authors include a thorough description of the problem, a review of the symptoms, a case study, how play therapy fits into overall treatment, and several interventions for that problem area with clear instructions and helpful graphics. In most chapters, ways of involving parents are included, as well as tips for teachers.

The background information in each chapter is succinct and useful, whether one is beginning a career in play therapy or has been practicing for a long time. I appreciate the reminders that this book provides that what we do is important and requires thoughtful attention to theoretical underpinnings as well as to the context in which the child lives so that our interventions will be effective. The interventions themselves are clearly presented. Some represent a new twist on an old game, while others offer completely novel ideas that can be used with a wide range of clients. I particularly liked the ideas for inexpensive prop-making for some of the techniques.

The organization of this book is noteworthy for the way it links interventions to problem areas in a very thoughtful, readable way. It is engaging and personable in style, written with intelligence and humor. It is a wonderful addition to the play therapy literature and valuable in its integration of key elements of quality play therapy with imaginative, effective, and playful ideas.

Risë VanFleet, PhD, RPT-S, CDBC
Family Enhancement & Play Therapy Center
International Institute for Animal Assisted Play Therapy™
Author of *Child-Centered Play Therapy; Animal Assisted Play Therapy*™;
*Filial Therapy: Strengthening Parent-Child Relationships Through Play*; and others
Boiling Springs, Pennsylvania

# Introduction

My passion for play therapy began as an undergraduate, where I was fortunate enough to have an internship at The Children's Center in Salt Lake City, Utah. It was through this experience that I had my first taste of the healing powers of play. I knew from this experience that I wanted to work with children and families, and sought out a graduate program at The University of Southern California that could enhance and support this through both academic rigor and clinical internships that could further facilitate my growing understanding and knowledge of this powerful healing process. Over the past 17 years, I have had the honor of being witness to countless children's stories and the process of healing. Play therapy works!

Play therapy gives words to the voiceless and power to the powerless. It is through play that healing can and does happen. One of the best parts of my job is watching a child learn how to smile and laugh again after experiencing unspeakable heartache. Throughout the years, I have also seen the power and importance of inviting the parents into the play therapy process from the beginning of treatment. You will find in this book that many of the interventions described are utilized to enhance, repair, and strengthen the bond of attachment between parent and child. The parent plays a crucial role in the healing process of their child, and it is important to keep in mind that a child can only make as much progress as their parent allows for, regardless of the diagnosis being treated.

When I began writing this book, I felt strongly that there needed to be more than just my own personal interventions that I have created over the years. I believe that two heads (or more!) are always better than one, and so I opened the door to my play therapy colleagues and invited different clinicians to contribute their own original play therapy interventions. Each of the interventions in this book is original and has not been published in other play therapy books.

## HOW TO USE THIS BOOK

This book is meant to be a resource and guidebook for clinicians who are working with children and families. It will inform the reader of not just the "tricks of the trade" and give useful, creative interventions, but will also enhance their understanding of mental health issues, risk factors involved, and the impact of the parent-child relationship within each disorder being treated. In order to be a *competent, confident* child clinician, it is crucial to understand not just *how* to treat a disorder, but *why* play therapy is effective and powerful. Clinicians need to understand the theoretical underpinnings of each intervention and be able to identify why they are using it and what they hope to achieve by utilizing a specific intervention with their child client.

In each chapter, we explore a specific diagnosis in terms of (1) typical, outward behavioral issues; (2) the impact on the family functioning; (3) the role of the parent in treatment; and (4) play therapy interventions that can be useful in treating this population. Although there are chapters that are dedicated to specific emotional and mental health issues, each diagnosis is also discussed in generalizable terms (for example, the chapter on anxiety is general in nature, but should be used to treat the specific diagnoses under that umbrella effectively). Many of the interventions in this book can be adapted to treat a wide range of emotional and behavioral issues of childhood.

It is my hope that this book will be a resource for both new and seasoned clinicians and will inspire you to seek out additional training in play therapy. I hope to ignite a passion inside of you to learn more about the proven powers of play therapy and begin incorporating these interventions in your treatment with children and families.

# Chapter 1 — What's the Big Deal About Play?

> *Play is a fun, enjoyable activity that elevates our spirits and brightens our outlook on life. It expands self-expression, self-knowledge, self-actualization, and self-efficacy. Play relieves feelings of stress and boredom, connects us to people in a positive way, stimulates creative thinking and exploration, regulates our emotions, and boosts our ego.*
>
> – Garry Landreth

In the world of play therapy, it is often said that **"Toys are used like words by children, and play is their language"** (Landreth, 2002, p. 16). Children explore, experience, and engage the world around them through play. How often have we watched a young child battling some ferocious monster and conquering this big beast, using all of their superhero powers and ninja moves? Or the child who mimics their parents or caregivers while playing house, saying the same words or calling out pet names? As a mother, I never was consciously aware that I said the word "Hon" until witnessing my young daughters playing, using this word interchangeably with "babe," "sweet pea," and "little one." *(How grateful I am that they didn't pick up on my other not so sweet language that sometimes slips out!)*

As one of the pioneers of child-centered play therapy, Garry Landreth asserts, "Play is a spontaneous, natural form of expression for children." Across gender, cultural, and ethnic lines, all children engage in play. The tools of play may be different, but this is the language of childhood. **In order to truly understand a child's world, we must be willing to enter into it, utilizing and learning their language.** We must be brave enough to just be present in it, not rush the child out of their comfort zone, their language, so we can feel comfortable back in our adult world and cognitive levels of understanding. This is a mistake many clinicians, even seasoned clinicians, make; they misunderstand how crucial it is that a child works in their own element, in their native tongue of play.

We have known of the power of play for centuries, with the ancient Greek philosophers and writers expounding on this topic. Plato wrote about the importance of play and opined that play is powerful and crucial for the developing child, as well as for their community at large. He wrote, "You can discover more about a person in an hour of play than in a year of conversation." During play, inhibition is lowered, laughter is increased, and freedom is released. For many, their true self comes out in the joy that comes from just being in the moment.

Play is commonly thought of as "child's work" but even through adulthood, play is crucial to our well-being and relationships. The language and nature of play changes as we age, but it is no less important in adulthood. Adults may play more in organized activities or sports, art, or physical activities. When there is spontaneity and laughter, play abounds. What happens in an adult romantic relationship when we stop playing? This is often when the relationship starts fizzling out or has become painful. We stop finding joy in one another without play. **This thing called play is necessary across the lifespan, from the first breath of a newborn child to the last breath of a life well-lived.** Play changes as we age, as does the language we use to describe play, but it is play all the same.

## HUMAN DEVELOPMENT

In developing infants, play is crucial for learning self-regulation as well as gross and fine motor development, and for developing a healthy attachment to their caregiver. Many clinicians are aware of Margaret Ainsworth's 1969 study known as the "Strange Situation," which studied the relationship of mothers and their babies. During the study, participants were filmed engaging and then disengaging with their infant child. What was discovered was shocking! When a mother would look at and engage with her child—cooing, tickling, touching the infant—the child would coo and smile back. As the mother responded to the infant's needs and emotions, the infant would maintain a regulated, happy, and comfortable state of being. However, if the mother looked at the child with an expressionless face, the infant would quickly become dysregulated, with drooling, crying, and agitation occurring within seconds of a non-responsive mother looking at them. This study was crucial in our understanding of attachment and how important the role of engagement and attunement is for the developing infant.

In later infanthood, play is crucial for developing object permanence, which translates to the knowledge of a secure attachment with their parent. A parent may playfully take away a toy or hide it behind them, and soon the baby begins to recognize that even though they can't see the rattle, it is there behind mother's back or under their blanket. Many babies will squeal in delight as they triumphantly find the missing object; in the process of doing so, they are developing crucial developmental tasks of learning and mastering object permanence.

Playing peek-a-boo is not just a way to play with a baby, but simultaneously creates bonds of attachment and teaches object permanence. As a baby learns that the father is still there behind his hands and pops out with a smile on his face, there is a joyful reunion between parent and child, and this teaches the baby, "You may not see me now, but I am here and coming back to you."

In later toddlerhood and preschool ages, play is how a child begins to make sense of the world around them. Children will begin to play out the themes of their environment, and by doing so, learn the necessary lessons of independence and self-mastery. Significant changes begin to happen in parent-child relationships in this developmental age, with many starting preschool or daycare. This is often the first time of an extended absence from their caregiver during the day. This is where an understanding of object permanence from their infant years is crucial to a child's well-being. A child learns, "I will be dropped off, but I know you will come back for me." Throughout the day, a child will spend much time using play to explore and understand the adult roles in their life, learn how to engage with others, and to develop imagination. Through play, a child can put on many different hats and experience feelings of empowerment, nurture, boldness, sadness, sickness, health, and empathy: all of which culminate and help a child create a sense of *self*.

## NEUROSCIENCE

We now know that the importance of play is essential for infants and their developing brains. Researchers began utilizing PET scans to view brain activity in the 1990's as that technology became available and accessible. What they found was shocking! Scientists discovered that more areas of the brain light up in neuroimaging studies when the participant is exposed to metaphor than any other form of human communication (Levin & Modell, 1997)! Exposure to metaphor and symbolism (i.e., *play)* has beneficial effects on brain development, as researchers have determined that this creates new neural pathways, helping the infant to develop social skills, emotional skills, communication skills, and relationship skills (Levin & Modell, 1997). When you are engaging in play, which in and of itself is symbolic metaphor in its truest form, whole parts of your brain are engaged, developing crucial connections that lead to a positive development of the child. More currently, researchers continue to discover how the brain processes emotions, affect, and experience into meaningful information. We have discovered how critical play is to a healthy development of the brain, as well as the negative impact of abuse, neglect, and trauma has on the developing brain. In Chapter 11 we will explore indepth how trauma impacts the brain, as well as how play is a restorative, healing mechanism to counteract this damaging experience.

## ATTACHMENT

Play is not only a fun, enjoyable activity, but a crucial attachment need as well. As we have discussed earlier, play is crucial in a child's physical and emotional development. Neuroscience has discovered that through play, bursts of oxytocin are released, which enhances our ability to form connections to others and bonds of attachment (Bartz, 2012). It is through play that the early attachment bond strengthens, and for some it is created for the first time between child and parent, creating the reciprocity needed for attunement and regulation (Shore, 1999).

*What is the difference between play and play therapy? How can playing with a bunch of toys be considered therapy? Isn't playing with toys in a therapy session and play therapy the same thing?*

These are questions many students and professionals alike have asked. The truth is that there are many key differences between playing and engaging in play therapy. Although play in and of itself has a therapeutic value, this does not necessarily constitute play therapy. This is a principle that many clinicians, young and old, fail to understand. In play therapy, a dance occurs between child and therapist as the child moves from phases of playing to therapeutic play to play therapy and back to play. We are often moving through these phases throughout the play therapy session. **The main difference between play and play therapy is the therapeutic intent and objective**. All play is inherently therapeutic; it is how we connect with others, engage in the world around us in wonder, and relieve stress and boredom. Play therapy is a specific therapeutic modality wherein a specially-trained mental health clinician harnesses the power of play and provides a therapeutic experience for the child (or adult) client.

We will dive into how and why play therapy works in the subsequent chapters. **I encourage you to read through the book (as each chapter builds upon the last) instead of skipping from topic to topic.** It is my hope that by the end of this book, you will feel more confident in your ability to implement play therapy into your practice, as well as become excited to learn more and become a certified Registered Play Therapist!

# Chapter 2 — How Play Therapy Works

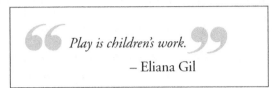

> *Play is children's work.*
> – Eliana Gil

Children are most often referred to play therapy when they are experiencing significant emotional and behavioral challenges that have begun to interfere with their daily functioning in home, school, and family life (Fine & Willingham, 2011). Referrals may come from sources such as parents, teachers, daycare centers, pediatricians, social workers, and case managers. **A child who may benefit from play therapy experiences a combination of the following symptoms:**

- Is not realizing full potential – academically or socially
- Has nightmares or disturbed sleep
- Is at risk for being (or is being) socially isolated at school
- Has suffered trauma (such as physical, emotional, or sexual abuse)
- Is (or is in the process of being) adopted or in foster care
- Parents are divorcing/separated
- Is suffering from anxiety, stress, or phobias
- Has suffered loss of any kind
- Is withdrawn or unhappy
- Is experiencing enuresis and/or encopresis
- Is autistic, disabled, or chronically ill
- Has difficulty in making and keeping friends
- Argues, frequently gets into fights with family and friends
- Bullies others or is bullied
- Displays inappropriate behaviors
- Experiences prejudice and/or discrimination
- Doesn't play

The Association for Play Therapy (2016) defines play therapy as:

*A systemic use of a theoretical model to establish an interpersonal process wherein trained play therapists use the therapeutic powers of play to help clients prevent or resolve psychosocial difficulties and achieve optimal growth and development.*

Schaefer and O'Conner explained this theory and therapeutic modality more clearly as, "Play therapy is an attempt to maximize the child's ability to engage in behavior which is fun, intrinsically complete, person-orientated, variable and/or flexible, non-instrumental and characterized by a natural flow"

(1983). Play therapists believe that children have an innate ability for resilience and have the tools they need to heal from whatever invisible (and sometimes visible) wounds they carry.

In play therapy, therapists are harnessing the power and language of play into a therapeutic model to promote mental health and healing in children young and old. There is a critical component of theory in play therapy, yet it is not confined to one particular theoretical orientation. At times, this may be confusing for some, as it is not a clear-cut model, with specific "rules" and guidelines. Landreth writes,

> *Play therapy is defined as a dynamic interpersonal relationship between a child (or person of any age) and a therapist trained in play therapy procedures who provides selected play materials and facilitates the development of a safe relationship for the child (or person of any age) to fully express and explore self (feelings, thoughts, experiences, and behaviors) through play, the child's natural medium of communication, for optimal growth and development"* (2002, p. 16).

Play therapy encompasses many variable theoretical models into one predominant belief that children have the innate ability to heal themselves, are resilient, and can be agents of change in and of themselves.

So, why do we need play therapists if children can do all of this on their own? Although a child has these inherent abilities to heal, they also need adult partners with them on their journey towards healing.

A play therapist is a licensed mental health clinician who has sought out specialized training in child development and in child and family therapy, as well as dedicated training in play therapy and the different modalities it encompasses. There is a strong element of necessary clinical supervision that has taken place, with a supervisor who is also a trained play therapist referred to as a Registered Play Therapist Supervisor (RPT-S). Mental health clinicians should only call themselves a "play therapist" if they have completed the necessary formal training and received the Registered Play Therapist (RPT) credential (in countries other than the United States of America, this credential may be called different names but the training requirements are very similar). For more information on becoming a Registered Play Therapist, please see the Association for Play Therapy website, www.a4pt.org.

## DIRECTIVE VERSUS NON-DIRECTIVE PLAY THERAPY

Depending upon the theoretical orientation, an individual clinician will more than likely have a preference for the type of play therapy to engage in with clients. **There are two main schools of thought regarding play therapy: directive and non-directive play therapy.** Directive play therapy is an approach that is predominantly a cognitive behavioral-based style of intervention that is highly structured in nature. Aaron Beck pioneered this approach in the 1960s as he developed cognitive behavioral therapy (CBT) for use in adults and could demonstrate this theory's effectiveness in child clients as well (Porter, Hernandez-Reif, & Jessee, 2009). The therapist identifies which play therapy supplies to use, directs the play, engages in processing questions, and overall is "in charge." In directive play, the main goal is to help the child develop healthy coping strategies to cope with life's challenges and struggles (Porter et al., 2009). Props, including puppets or stuffed animals, as well as a wide variety of play materials, are used to assist the therapist and child to develop a positive outlook, healthy coping skills, and improve behavioral concerns.

Many people in the early stages of play therapist training feel most comfortable with this approach, as often the interventions are more manualized and easy to replicate – much like the interventions you will find throughout this workbook. Directive play therapy is highly beneficial when facilitating play therapy-based groups or family therapy sessions, as it offers a structured activity-based style of intervention and facilitation. It is a preferred treatment modality in working with a child struggling with anxiety, separation anxiety, and trauma issues (Porter et al., 2009).

Non-directive play therapy differs significantly from directive play therapy. When utilizing a non-directive approach, the therapist is primarily an observer in the play (but may be a participant if the child invites the therapist to be part of the experience) as well as an integral part of the play therapy process. This type of intervention is child-centered, meaning that the child is "in charge" and leads the play with little input or direction from the therapist. The child directs the play and instructs the therapist as to what, if any, role to play. Safety boundaries are in place, such as "Everybody needs to be safe" or "No hurting me or you." The therapist is there to provide safety, understanding, and security, but not to guide the play activity (Landreth, 2002, Porter et al., 2009).

Virginia Axline developed the Eight Principles of Play Therapy in 1947, and these continue to serve as guidelines for many who practice child-centered play therapy. The principles are as follows (Axline, 1947; Porter et al., 2009):

1. Develop a friendly relationship with the child.
2. Accept the child without question.
3. Establish a permissive relationship so that the child feels they may express their feelings freely.
4. Recognize and reflect the feelings that the child is expressing.
5. Maintain respect for the child's problem-solving skills.
6. Let the child lead and refrain from directing the child's actions.
7. Let the session progress naturally, without an agenda.
8. Make limitations that are only necessary to make the child aware of his/her responsibility in the patient-therapist relationship.

Many therapists may feel intimidated by the non-directive approach to play therapy, as it requires significant presence of the therapist (Crenshaw & Kenney-Noziska, 2014). You are never more intimately involved in the play therapy process than when you are utilizing a child-centered model. You must be fully present with the child in this approach and trust that the healing power of play and the therapeutic relationship will work. Learning to trust the process and becoming trained in this approach is something that takes time to develop but is an important clinical skill when working with young children.

## PUTTING PLAY THERAPY INTO PRACTICE

It is important to have a parent (or guardian) consultation prior to meeting with the child. I require a parent consultation without the child present prior to beginning therapeutic services with a child, as it offers a chance to have a candid conversation about the difficulties the child and parent are experiencing, as well as gives an opportunity for the clinician to set expectations for confidentiality, treatment goal-setting, and parental involvement. During this consultation, it is important for the clinician to learn as much as possible about not only the presenting reason for referral, but also a developmental history of the child, including previous therapeutic interventions and evaluations, and medical, social, family, and school history (Fine & Willingham, 2011). By providing parents with education about the assessment and relationship-building process, a clinician can begin to establish a therapeutic alliance with the parent, which is key to helping the child reach success.

I recommend scheduling out at least six therapy sessions that are consecutive and consistent, ideally on a weekly basis held at the same time for each therapy session. This provides continuity in the therapeutic process, as well as helps to decrease the anxiety of attending counseling services for both the child and the parent. Providing parents with education about the assessment and relationship-building process not only helps them learn, but also helps establish a key element of the therapeutic alliance with the parents, as well as with the child.

Although many therapists must give a mental health diagnosis after the first visit for insurance and billing purposes, in reality, the assessment period is much longer than one individual session. The primary goal of the initial play therapy session with the child present is to establish rapport and help the child feel comfortable in the playroom environment and with the therapist (Landreth, 2002). The following two sessions are the assessment period, as this gives time for the child to build a relationship and act as their true self. Many children in the early stages of treatment are either on their very best or very worst behaviors, depending upon the reason for referral. **Setting realistic, developmentally-appropriate expectations for both child and parent is crucial for building a therapeutic alliance.** Educating parents that the assessment period is the first three sessions helps alleviate pressure demands on the therapist, and allows time to build a therapeutic alliance.

Ideally, play therapists have access to a large, well-stocked playroom full of selected toys for the child to choose from. However, many clinicians who practice play therapy have agency and budget constraints that may limit their ability to have separate healing space outside of their traditional office space. I encourage those practicing in this type of a clinical setting to designate an area of their office to be dedicated to play therapy and toy storage. With Pinterest® at your fingertips, there are countless creative ways of creating storage that are still aesthetically appealing. I also encourage readers to visit my YouTube channel (search "Clair Mellenthin" on YouTube) and watch *Building a Portable Playroom*. You can access it through this link: https://www.youtube.com/watch?v=v4SCfrGYEeM

## TOOLS OF A PLAY THERAPIST

The most important tools of a play therapist are creativity and flexibility; toys and other materials won't help a child if the play therapist isn't innovative and strategic about how they are used. Still, recent research has outlined specific toys and categories of toys that are invaluable and should be staples in a play therapist's clinical setting (Ray et al., 2013; Kottman, 2013).

Based on Terry Kottman's five categories of the toys, the following are offered as suggestions for building your playroom:

| FAMILY/NURTURING TOYS | dolls, dollhouse, baby dolls, bottles, kitchen set, utensils, pretend food, puppets, sand in a sandbox |
|---|---|
| SCARY TOYS | reptiles, dinosaurs, insects, spiders, snakes, dragons, puppets with "fierce" expressions |
| AGGRESSIVE TOYS | swords, guns, knives, handcuffs, shields, rope, toy soldiers, tanks, Bop Bag |
| EXPRESSIVE TOYS | paint, play-dough, clay, crayons, markers, scissors, craft supplies, feathers, egg cartons, paper, tape |
| PRETEND/FANTASY TOYS | dress-up clothes, wands, fairy wings, masks, jewelry, telephones, doctor's kit, zoo animals, blocks |

Clinicians often worry about the costs of building their play therapy room. While there are essential toys you need to have to begin with, Garry Landreth has offered shrewd advice, as he has cautioned therapists to *select* toys, not *collect* toys. As you will see in my YouTube video *How to Build a Portable Playroom,* your toy must-haves do not have to take up a lot of space or cost a lot of money. Remember, the most important toy is YOU and your ability to be flexible and creative.

# Chapter 3 — Play Therapy Interventions for Attention Deficit Hyperactivity Disorder

> " *To think things through, children need to play things through.* "
>
> – Jean Piaget

Attention Deficit Hyperactivity Disorder (ADHD) affects over 2 million children within the United States (Portrie-Bethke, Hill, & Bethke, 2009). Children who have been diagnosed with ADHD experience elevated levels of impulsivity, hyperactivity, and inattention that can impair their daily functioning, which is the leading cause for students in the school setting to be referred to counseling or to see the school psychologist (Ray, Schottelkorb, & Tsai, 2007).

## ADHD Symptoms

- **Inattention:** struggles to pay attention for long periods of time, will often daydream or "check out" at school/during activities
- **Excessive stimulation:** constantly in motion, bouncing their legs, tapping on things, licking objects, touching others
- **Hyperactivity:** easily aroused and dysregulated, struggles with limit-setting and appropriate physical responses (many parents and teachers will describe this as bouncing off the walls)
- **Irritability:** gets frustrated easily, overwhelmed, emotional dysregulation
- **Inability to delay gratification:** difficulty accepting "no," waiting their turn
- **Impulsiveness:** interrupts others, has difficulty waiting their turn, blurts out answers or thoughts, acts without thinking of consequences, makes simple mistakes because child not thinking through question before answering
- **Overactivity:** restlessness, inability to sit still, fidgeting, constant movement
- Problems with executive functioning, problem-solving, making and accomplishing goals, arousal
- **Organization deficits:** difficulty staying focused, struggling to remember where they put things or what they were doing, turning in homework, messiness, distraction, often off-task
- **Relationship deficits:** Learning disabilities common as is poor school performance, peer and family relationship problems, oppositional and defiant problematic behaviors, authority conflicts, can channel focus onto stimulating, interesting activities of their choice (e.g., video games), sleep disturbances, risk of negative adolescent/adult outcomes

Many children are not diagnosed with ADHD until they enter the school years, as many of the social and emotional struggles they are experiencing are also typical of the developmental phases of toddlerhood and preschool ages. However, parents often share that they have always felt that their child was very difficult to parent and very "busy" during these early stages in the developmental history taking. Parents also report that even in infanthood, their child engaged in higher levels of sensory seeking and stimulation, was difficult to soothe, and had a hard time connecting and forming a secure bond. Many children diagnosed with ADHD also have a history of struggling with adapting to change, aggressiveness, higher frustration levels, and at times, physical problems including higher rate of injury and motor coordination problems (Kronenberger & Meyer, 2001). These issues can have a significantly detrimental impact on the parent-child relationship.

When treating a child's ADHD, it is important to look beyond the external behavioral issues and address the underlying low self-esteem and poor relationships with family members, peers, and teachers in the clinical treatment plan. The child often feels rejected, lonely, discouraged, and worthless. Many children with an ADHD diagnosis struggle with limited social skills (which will be addressed in Chapter 10) and are often unaware of how their negative or attention-seeking behaviors impact those around them. If they *are* aware, they may feel confused and lack understanding of what they are doing that pushes others away or feel unable to stop.

The behavioral and emotional issues connected to ADHD correlate to the child's inability to meet the social, emotional, and interpersonal demands of life in an age-appropriate manner, and they often act much younger than their chronological age (Kaduson, 2006b). In fact, studies have shown that children diagnosed with ADHD possess age-appropriate cognitive skills (and sometimes higher than above average intelligence), but their emotional maturity is about one-third their chronological age (Kaduson, 2006b; Barkley, 2000; Mrug, Hoza, & Gerdes, 2001). For example, a child may have advanced math skills but have a hard time deciphering social cues with peers, while regularly engaging in behaviors that a younger child would do when overwhelmed or upset.

# Case Study — Jimmy

Jimmy is an eight-year-old child recently diagnosed with ADHD. He is small for his age and struggles with making and keeping friends. He often will annoy his peers by touching or poking them, taking their things without asking, or by his impulsive behaviors in class. His teacher regularly gives him a yellow or red card for not listening or doing what he is supposed to do in his classroom. His parents report that since he was a toddler, Jimmy has been a handful; he is constantly getting into things, accidentally breaking things, dumping out cereal boxes, or taking a long time to complete a simple request. He struggles to fall and stay asleep, and he often gets out of bed numerous times before he settles down. Sometimes there is an excuse, such as needing a drink of water or needing to go to the bathroom; other times, his parents will find him fiddling with some gadget or toy that he is not supposed to be playing with. Jimmy has told his mother, "My brain never turns off! My body will be so tired, but my brain is wide awake and keeps me up even when I want to go to sleep."

Jimmy's parents sought out counseling after the third time his teacher called due to his behavioral issues in class. His teacher informed them that while Jimmy was a good student and nice to others, his behavioral challenges were getting in the way of other students learning (as well as posing a problem to himself socially). Children were beginning to shy away from him or not want to play with him. Because he was constantly getting into trouble in the classroom, his peers were beginning to tease him or call him "the bad kid." At home, his parents were feeling exasperated and frustrated with his lack of follow-through and his impulsivity.

Jimmy was referred to play therapy. At his first session, he came into the playroom and immediately began rummaging through drawers and bins of toys. He would take out one toy and play with it for a few minutes before becoming distracted and getting another toy or game out. He continued to do this until the session was over, bouncing from one activity to another without finishing a game or completing a drawing. He talked incessantly to his therapist and did not take a break from chatting the entire 45 minutes! After the initial assessment and parent consultation, it was decided that Jimmy would benefit from a blend of individual and family-based play therapy.

Throughout the first few sessions, Jimmy appeared slightly dysregulated, but was cheerful and engaged with his play therapist. He had a difficult time staying focused on one task or activity and would jump from sand to puppets to paints back to sand throughout the play therapy sessions. Jimmy especially enjoyed the sand and would run his fingers back and forth through it; this would appear to settle him down. His therapist began teaching him self-regulating and calming skills that he could use when he felt the impulse to jump up, get out of his seat, or poke the person next to him. He and his parents made a Calm Down Jar in family play therapy and practiced sitting still and watching the glitter float down to the bottom of the jar. Jimmy loved to shake the jar and then watch the glitter slowly swirl down.

In one family play session, Jimmy created a sand tray of what his ADHD felt like inside. This was an eye-opening moment for his parents, as they had been more focused on their frustrations and the outward behavioral challenges, but had not had the insight to recognize how chaotic and disorganized their child felt internally. This led to a greater level of empathy from the parents; as they began to see the world through their child's eyes, they started to recognize when they could step in and when they should step out and allow Jimmy the opportunity to learn from his experiences.

As Jimmy learned healthier coping skills, he and his parents were better able to communicate and listen to one another, which helped their relationship to improve significantly. His parents felt much less frustration and helplessness, and they were much more attuned to Jimmy's emotional needs. This helped Jimmy to regulate and learn ways to manage and control his impulsivity.

## PARENTAL INVOLVEMENT

Including the parent(s) in the therapeutic process is critical, as they often feel overwhelmed, embarrassed, frustrated, and emotionally disconnected from their child. The behavioral issues can be extremely challenging, and parents often feel shame over their inability to put a stop to the negative behaviors. They may also feel rejected by their child, as the child is unable to listen to or modify and correct their behaviors. This in turn may lead to a reject-reject cycle in their relationship, meaning that as the parents feel rejected or unwanted, they may pull away emotionally and, in turn, reject their child. This may be either intentional or completely an unconscious act. This sense of rejection then leads the child to act out or pull away emotionally, leaving the parents feeling rejected and hurt. In this vicious cycle between parents and child, significant pain and attachment wounding may occur, with the result of the child feeling worthless or unlovable.

When children feel worthless, inadequate, and discouraged, they may act out to gain attention or feel like they have a sense of power (Portrie-Bethke et al., 2009). Repairing the parent-child relationship is crucial for change to happen within the family system and elsewhere. It is also critical for parents to understand what their child's inner world looks like and feels like, to develop empathy and compassion for the struggles the child is experiencing. By educating parents about this disorder (including the underlying self-esteem and self-worth issues, brain development, and emotional development), they are better able to set appropriate limits and expectations, effectively manage the misbehavior, and form a more secure relationship with their child.

## PLAY THERAPY AND ADHD

Play therapy is an appropriate treatment for ADHD, as it involves the child in the process and can teach the child life management techniques, help the child to better understand his/her behaviors and underlying emotional needs, learn healthy coping skills, increase delayed gratification skills, and improve the parent-child relationship. Play therapy can also improve communication patterns that can help parents to develop insight into their own needs as well as the needs of their child (Portrie-Bethke et al., 2009). Because children with ADHD generally have such high sensory-seeking needs and attention deficits, play therapy interventions need to be dynamic, action-orientated, and beyond traditional talk therapy (Portrie-Bethke et al., 2009; Kaduson, 2006b).

A playful, dynamic approach to therapy will help to engage the child more effectively, as well as begin to teach impulse-control, focus, and concentration skills. It is also important to include clear limit-setting in all the interventions employed, as this can enhance the relationship development, as well as set a clear understanding of the rules and eliminate destructive behaviors in the playroom and in their interpersonal relationships (Portrie-Bethke et al., 2009). Many of the interventions in this chapter can be modified for individual, family, or group therapy. In Chapter 10, many of the play therapy interventions can also be utilized in the treatment of ADHD and adapted for individual and family therapy.

## SPECIAL NOTE TO TEACHERS

Schoolteachers often bear the brunt of ADHD and feel unequipped and untrained to handle the emotional and behavioral challenges this disorder causes. Some useful tips to manage the classroom and a child diagnosed with ADHD include:

1. **Have the Child Help (When Possible)**

   A child with ADHD can be a great classroom helper! The child needs to get up and move regularly, which can be a challenge in a traditional classroom. One way to help with this issue is to make the child your "special helper" and have him/her take "important" messages to the office at least once a day. Your message may say "have a great day" to the secretary or it may be the lunch count or however creative you feel like being that morning. The important part of this exercise is this will (1) increase the child's self-esteem, (2) get the wiggles out, and (3) improve behaviors until recess.

2. **Give Permission for the Child to Have One Fidget Toy**

   Allowing for some type of fidget toy can be useful so long as the child can keep it to him/herself. A small stress ball or some type of textured fabric can be a great asset in helping the child pay attention and keep their hands to themselves. A useful idea is to put a very large rubber band on the bottom of the desk between the legs that the child can bounce his/her feet on. Paradoxically, these small distractions help the child to focus, not play with other students' possessions, and relieve the internal pressure and need to move.

3. **Get Up and MOVE!**

   This is helpful for everybody in your class – especially YOU! At the start of the day, get the kids jumping up and down, or have a three-minute dance party in between subjects. This helps get the blood flowing, oxygen moving, and brains rewired to focus on the next subject.

4. **Teach Your Class How to Use the Lemon Squeezies (Chapter 4)**

   Everyone can benefit from a five-minute guided full-body relaxation, especially the child whose body never stops moving!

5. **Don't Take Away Recess as Punishment**

   Never take away recess from your student with ADHD! This is a crucial time for both you and the child to breathe, move, and take a break. If the child needs some sort of disciplinary action due to acting out or other misbehavior, or if peer conflict requires more supervision, still allow the child to go outside and take a break. If needed, have an adult on hand to supervise (not you! You need a break too!) or to give attention to the child, but everybody needs recess time to reset and recharge. Taking away recess from a child with ADHD is like taking away the air to breathe!

In the following pages, several play therapy interventions that are useful in treating ADHD are provided. Many of these interventions can be adapted for use in individual, family, group therapy, and social skills classes. It is important to remember to utilize a variety of big motor play and use of mindfulness is important in your treatment planning.

# RED LIGHT, GREEN LIGHT

Impulse control and delayed gratification are two skills children with ADHD struggle with significantly. This play therapy intervention addresses these issues by teaching the child how to stop and wait their turn, as well as stand still in order to "win." This is also a very playful activity to use in family therapy sessions to address the underlying attachment needs of the family members to reach "home base." (In subsequent family therapy sessions, you may want to use the metaphor of "home base" to describe feeling safe, accepted, and secure with one another.) You may use the Stop and Go signs to represent different challenges the family has faced and overcome, as well as to demonstrate how to keep rebounding from hard times and experiences.

## SUPPLIES NEEDED:

> Masking tape
> Red marker, green marker
> Large tongue depressors
> Elmer's Glue
> Printable Stop and Go signs (provided on page 15)

**Note:** It is helpful to do this activity in a large space, free of obstacles or distractions.

## DIRECTIONS:

1. Cut out the printable Stop and Go signs. Instruct the child to color the Stop sign red and the Go sign green.

2. Glue or tape a tongue depressor to each sign.

3. At one end of the room, use the masking tape to make a long strip across the floor, designating Home Base. On the other end of the room, tape another long strip of tape to the floor designating the Start Line.

4. Instruct the child how to play Red Light, Green Light. Each person will take a turn being "It" and oversee the Stop and Go signs. This person turns their back to the group or family members standing at the Start Line. They hold up one sign at a time. The goal of the family members is to get to Home Base as fast as they can, without touching the person who is It. Whoever gets there first "wins" and gets to take the next turn overseeing the signs.

5. When the red Stop sign is shown, all players must stop (freeze) and hold whatever position they may be in until the green Go sign is shown. The person who is It needs to have their back turned away from the group. If a person is unable to hold their position during the Stop sign, they must go back to the Start Line and start over.

6. Allow for everybody to have a turn being "It," and then discuss what it felt like to be in charge, to not be able to see where people were standing or moving, as well as how it felt to have to go back and start over.

7. Explain that just like a red Stop sign tells us to stop, sometimes kids will engage in "red" behaviors, which are behaviors that can cause negative emotional or social consequences. Kids may also engage in "green" behaviors, which are positive, pro-social behaviors that receive positive attention from others.

8. Have the child write down three red behaviors. For example: Tapping on my neighbor's desk at school, kicking the wall when I feel mad, not looking when I cross the street.

9. Have the child write down three green behaviors. For example: Telling my Mom, "I love you," or saying, "Okay, I'm sharing my toys with my little brother."

10. Give the child the signs to take home for the child and parents to play red light, green light throughout the week. Encourage the parent to "catch the child being good" by giving praise whenever they see green light behaviors.

## Worksheet

# RED LIGHT, GREEN LIGHT

My **STOP** (red) behaviors this week were:

1. _____

2. _____

3. _____

4. _____

5. _____

6. _____

7. _____

8. _____


My **GO** (green) behaviors this week were:

1. _____

2. _____

3. _____

4. _____

5. _____

6. _____

7. _____

8. _____

# WIGGLE FIDGETS

Wiggle fidgets help the child get the wiggles out in a healthy, pro-social manner. Many kids with ADHD have unique sensory-seeking behaviors including touching, tapping, licking, kicking, etc., that usually annoy those around them, as these behaviors can be very distracting and bothersome. By creating a Wiggle Fidget Box, children with ADHD can channel their need for exploration and stimulation in a way that meets their sensory needs and does not cause distress to those around them.

Over time, the therapist and child create "tools" to add to their wiggle fidgets that the child can use to help calm their body, get the wiggles out, and improve family relationships. It is useful to discuss with the teacher at school how some of the wiggle fidgets could be adapted to the classroom, for example, gluing Velcro® to the bottom of the child's desk so they can run their fingers across the textures instead of jumping out of their seats or bothering others nearby.

Note: The Velcro® is glued side by side so the child does not rip the strips apart, causing noise and distraction. This is a quiet wiggle fidget!

## SUPPLIES NEEDED:

Shoebox (any size)
Three to six inches of Velcro®
A variety of ribbons (different textures and lengths), pipe cleaners, different textured material scraps
Hot glue gun and hot glue sticks

You may add to the inside of the box: stress ball, silly putty, liquid motion toy, calm down jar, spinning top, etc.

## DIRECTIONS:

1. On the outside of the shoebox, instruct the child to determine where to glue the fabric, Velcro®, ribbons, etc. The adult (parent or therapist) will glue where directed. Cover the shoebox with different textures and sensory-seeking stimuli.

2. Practice rubbing and touching the different material on the outside of the box, processing how each texture feels to the child – is it stimulating or soothing?

3. Instruct the child and parent to take home the wiggle fidget box to use when they need to calm down their body, seek out sensory stimuli, or cope with overwhelming emotions. This is also useful at bedtime to help relax and soothe.

4. Parents should be instructed that the wiggle fidgets should not be used as a punitive measure – either due to misbehavior ("You didn't listen, so you have to use your wiggle fidgets for 10 minutes") or having their soothing toys taken away because of misbehavior ("You were naughty at the store, so you don't get your wiggle fidgets tonight").

5. Throughout treatment, you may create new soothing or stimulating wiggle fidgets to add to your client's wiggle fidget box. Items such as stress balls, Rubik's Cubes, pinwheels, rubber bands, and silly putty can be very helpful. Be creative, and have fun!

# CALM DOWN JAR

A Calm Down Jar is very useful for many of the emotional and behavioral issues often found with children diagnosed with ADHD, as well as with young individuals experiencing anxiety and trauma-related disorders. The child is able to practice calming down the body and regulating him/herself, breathing in long, slow breaths as the glitter floats to the bottom of the jar. Shaking, squeezing, turning, and watching the jar as the glitter settles allows the body to receive sensory input needed to organize thoughts and focus attention, as well as allowing the child to "rewire" their nervous system as they learn to regulate their breathing and emotional state while taking long, deep breaths. This activity helps to increase the child's coping skill of calming themselves when feeling anxious, overstimulated, overwhelmed, and tired. It is also a great tool to put into the Wiggle Fidget Box!

## SUPPLIES NEEDED:

Small jar with a lid (such as a baby food jar or small plastic water bottle)
Glitter
Clear glue or glitter glue
Food coloring
Duct tape
Hot water
Small whisk

**Note:** It may be desirable to use a plastic bottle if there are developmental, anger, or impulse-control concerns, so the jar is less likely to break.

## DIRECTIONS:

**1.** Pour hot water into the jar and fill until there is a one- to two-inch gap at the top. Add two tablespoons of the clear or glitter glue. Whisk (or shake) together until glue is dissolved. Be careful with small children if using hot water. The adult may want to shake the bottle to protect small hands.

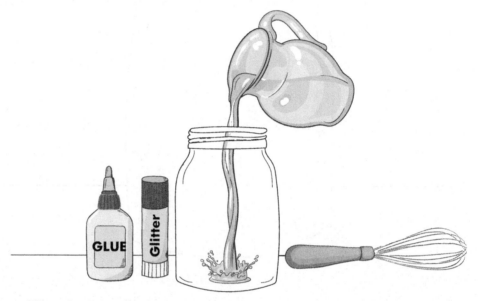

**2.** Add glitter, filling the bottom of the jar about half an inch. (You can also put in sequins, small plastic toys, pine needles, etc.)

**3.** Add a few drops of food coloring.

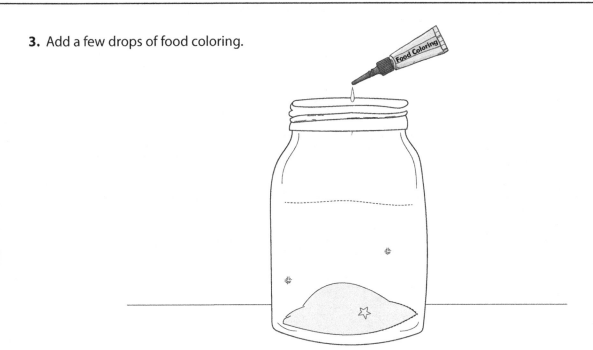

**4.** Screw on lid and duct tape shut.

**5.** Shake the jar and watch the glitter float down to the bottom. The child may shake it as much as they want. As the glitter settles, instruct the child to take long, slow, deep breaths. Use a timer to time the child sitting still as the glitter is settling. You can play "beat the clock," lengthening the time the child sits still, with the child earning a point every time they can lengthen their score.

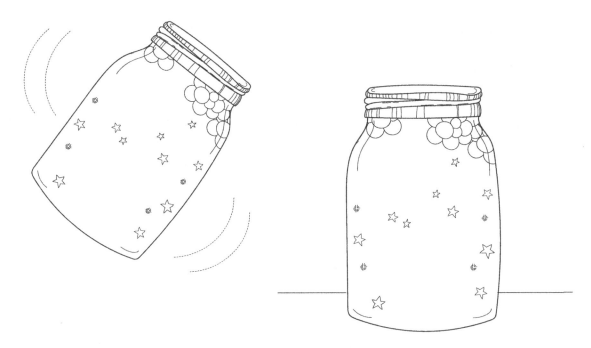

**6.** The child takes home their Calm Down Jar and can use it throughout the week to practice sitting still, calming down their body and getting the wiggles out in a socially appropriate manner.

**Chapter 4** — # Play Therapy Interventions for Anxiety Disorders

>  *When you're free, you can play and when you're playing, you become free.*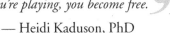
> — Heidi Kaduson, PhD

Anxiety is used to describe an intense feeling of worry, fear, and nervousness. These worries can cause a feeling of helplessness and powerlessness, as well as feeling overwhelmed. When these feelings begin to impair your ability to function in your everyday life, they can be diagnosed as a disorder. Anxiety disorders are one of the most common childhood mental health diagnoses, affecting about 12%–20% of the U.S. population (Knell & Dasari, 2006). Included in childhood-based anxiety disorders are Separation Anxiety Disorder (SAD), Panic Disorder, Specific Phobia, Social Anxiety Disorder, and Generalized Anxiety Disorder (GAD). Obsessive-Compulsive Disorder (OCD) is also an anxiety disorder, but will be covered in a separate chapter in this workbook due to some of the complexity surrounding this particular anxiety disorder. **All of the play therapy interventions explained in this chapter can be modified to use with children and adolescents who have been diagnosed with one or more of the anxiety disorders**.

In childhood, worry and anxiety are often part of the normal process of development (Knell & Dasari, 2006). Toddlers and preschool-age children who are beginning to experience the amazing power of imagination can suddenly imagine that there are monsters under the bed, and what was once a cozy, safe place to snuggle and go to sleep is now filled with fear and uncertainty. Nighttime struggles are a constant in most families in this developmental stage, at times baffling to the parent, especially when a child has a sudden onset of nighttime fears. When normal childhood fears begin to impair the child's ability to function in their daily lives and relationships, it is useful to seek out additional support and resources.

In older childhood, worry is a normal part of development as the child continues to stretch their comfort zones as school, friends, playdates, daycare, and sports begin to be included as part of their daily schedule. Worry may turn into fear and anxiety during this time, however. The changing structure of the American school system may contribute to the development of a child's anxiety, as there are now secure entrances or metal detectors in many schools across the county due to school-based violence and the fear of mass shootings. This anxiety within the school system can trickle down to the students, as children in schools now not only have fire and earthquake drills, but also armed intruder drills! Though most of us would agree that these safety precautions are a good thing, it's easy to see how these changes could cause anxiety in anybody, but especially in a younger child who may not have been exposed to these concerns and possibilities prior to attending school.

There are key differences between fear, worry, and anxiety. Fear is a biological response rooted in the fight/flight response in our primitive brain. It usually is a response to a legitimate danger. An example of this is running away from a dangerous situation; for example, if you were hiking and came across a rattlesnake on the path, you would stop, turn around, and run the other direction away from the poisonous snake. Our brains are wired to protect us and help us to escape and protect ourselves.

**Worry, on the other hand, is a concern that something bad could happen; if may or may not be based on real or past experience.** A child may worry that there is a monster under the bed, bringing up the fear that something bad *could* happen to them in the middle of the night. Anxiety is often a learned response that usually occurs in the absence of real danger or in response to a perceived threat (Knell & Dasari, 2006). Children who experience anxiety are constantly worried and their worries feel like they are on a runaway train – with the worst-case scenario of every worry they may have playing out in their minds. Now this monster who lives under the bed is not only going to gobble them up in the middle of the night, but everyone they love, too! In fact, this monster may not even wait until nighttime to feast on the family, but could pop out at any moment when the parent turns away! Researchers have found that it is very common for anxious adults to produce anxious children, parenting them in an anxious, fear-based model which often leads to the parents removing the child from situations that *could be* anxiety-provoking, resulting in the child never really learning how to regulate their emotions or learn healthy coping strategies to combat their anxiety symptoms (Hannesdottir & Ollendick, 2007).

**A concept to help understand anxiety is thinking of this as a false alarm that is constantly going off, leaving the child in a constant state of hypervigilance, hyperarousal, fear, and worry.** The brain "tricks" the child into believing or worrying that there is a real threat looming and they need to protect themselves, often employing maladaptive coping strategies rooted in avoidance, aggression, and emotional dysregulation.

| Anxiety Symptoms | |
|---|---|
| | 1. Excessive worry |
| | 2. Restlessness |
| | 3. Irritability |
| | 4. Difficulty concentrating |
| | 5. Tension |
| | 6. Sleep problems |
| | 7. Hyperarousal |
| | 8. Overly serious manner |
| | 9. Perfectionism/overachievement |
| | 10. Constant seeking of reassurance |
| | 11. Somatic complaints (headaches, stomachaches, dizzy spells, etc.) |
| | 12. Self-consciousness |
| | 13. School avoidance |

## PLAY THERAPY AND ANXIETY

Play therapy is an effective treatment modality for childhood anxiety because it is developmentally sensitive, and it allows that child to experience exposure to their fear in a safe, contained space. In play therapy, the child can "practice" feeling brave, learning healthy coping strategies, improving communication and emotional intelligence, as well as self-regulation skills. Including the parent in the assessment and treatment of an anxious child is also paramount in helping to create lasting change in the family system, which may be perpetuating the child's anxiety.

# Case Study — Miguel

Miguel is a 10-year-old child who was recently referred to counseling due to deteriorating grades, increasing social isolation, verbal aggression, and significant weight loss over the space of a few months. Previously, Miguel's parents report that he has always been an outgoing, social child who loves spending time with family and friends, excels at school, and is one of the top soccer players in his competition team. He demands perfection of himself and will spend hours after school practicing soccer drills over and over even when he does not have practice scheduled. Recently, his parents were informed by his teacher that Miguel has not turned in homework for weeks, will become highly agitated during math and spelling tests, and will rip up his papers in frustration during class.

Miguel was recently moved down from the top spelling group to the grade level group in his class. He views this as a huge disappointment and failure, even though his parents have tried to reassure him that they only care if he is trying his best and grades are not the most important thing. His mother informed the therapist that she has found several completed homework assignments in Miguel's backpack, and when asked why he hasn't turned them in, Miguel will begin to cry and say, "It isn't good enough." His father remarked that he has noticed that his son always looks tired in the morning and has increasingly developed large, dark circles under his eyes even though bedtime is at a reasonable hour and he should be getting plenty of sleep.

Miguel was referred for play therapy to address the anxiety symptoms he has been exhibiting at home, school, and in his personal relationships. When Miguel first began play therapy, he requested the presence of his mother or father in the playroom with him, as he felt too anxious to be alone with the therapist (this turned out to be beneficial; the family relationship struggles had compounded Miguel's anxiety symptoms, and family-based play therapy could immediately commence from the beginning of the counseling sessions). Miguel expressed feeling anxious about not being a good enough student, a good enough son and brother, and worried that he was a disappointment to his parents because he had received lower grades in school, missed a goal during a game, or lost his temper at home. Even with his parents reassuring him that he was loved and important, he constantly was looking for "evidence" that they viewed him as a failure. Consequently, his parents felt like they were being constantly scrutinized for giving any indication that their son wasn't good enough, thus straining their relationship with him.

Miguel disclosed during therapy that he often spent hours lying awake at night worrying about school and how he would perform on tests, homework, and if his friends at school really liked him. He worried that his coach would replace him on the team if he wasn't the very best player. During one play therapy session, Miguel created a Worry Catcher, which helped him to learn healthy coping strategies to calm his anxiety and worries, replacing them with positive thoughts or learning how to "toss them out the window." Miguel was taught the Lemon Squeezies to calm his body down at night or whenever he was feeling stressed or overwhelmed. One intervention that was particularly powerful towards the end of therapy was Stars and Dots, used to help decrease Miguel's negative self-talk and improve self-esteem, as well as strengthen the parent-child relationship (for detailed instructions on the play therapy intervention Stars and Dots, please see Chapter 9). Miguel and his parents engaged in the play therapy throughout the several weeks Miguel attended counseling services.

# LEMON SQUEEZIES
# GUIDED RELAXATION

Lemon Squeezies is a full body guided relaxation technique that involves guided imagery, as well as teaching how to *feel* your body and *calm* it simultaneously. When a child can learn how to calm their body, they can learn to calm their mind, regulate their breathing, and take back control from their worry and anxiety. This intervention is also very useful and effective when working with children who have been exposed to trauma. This specific intervention is adapted from a Trauma Focused-CBT intervention found in the TF-CBT course at www.musc.edu. The original creator of Lemon Squeezies is unknown.

## SUPPLIES NEEDED:

> Blank puzzle
> Markers

## DIRECTIONS:

Instruct your client to close his/her eyes and begin taking long, deep breaths. Tell the child to practice breathing in through the nose and exhaling through the mouth. You may want to count to five on each inhale and exhale to allow for deep belly breathing. The client may either sit or lay down, however he/she is most comfortable.

***Guided Imagery: The therapist will read this script to the child as they are in a relaxed state of being.***

*Today, we are going to learn how to relax our bodies from our heads to our toes. Listen to my voice and follow along with me if you would like to. If you come to parts you don't like, you don't have to go there. Just listen to my voice, follow along, and let's begin our journey.*

*I want you to imagine you are holding a lemon in your left hand. Can you smell the lemon? Can you imagine how it would feel to hold this lemon in your hand? Now I want you to imagine we are going to make lemonade today with this lemon and we are going to squeeze it to get every drop of lemon juice out of it. Ready? Squeeze! Squeeze harder, harder (pause for about five seconds). You can relax your hand. Now I want you to imagine we are going to squeeze this same lemon again to get more juice out of it. Ready? Squeeze! Squeeze harder, harder (pause about five seconds). Okay, good job. You can relax your hand. Now, we need to get just a little more juice into our lemonade and are going to squeeze another lemon. Can you feel it in your hand? Ready? Squeeze! Squeeze harder, as hard as you can (pause about five seconds)! Okay, great job. You can relax your hand and shake it out if you need to. You really squeezed that lemon tight. We got almost all of the juice we needed to make our tasty lemonade.*

*Now, we are going to do the same thing using our right hand. I want you to imagine you are holding another lemon in your right hand. Are you ready to squeeze it? Can you smell the sweet lemon scent? Can you feel the soft, bumpy lemon peel? We are going to finish making our lemonade now. Ready? Squeeze with your right hand. Tighter, tighter . . . (pause about five seconds). Okay, good. You can let go and relax your hand. We need to squeeze some more juice though, ready? Squeeze! Harder, harder (pause about five seconds). Good job! You can relax your hand. We are almost there. Are you ready to drink some of our yummy lemonade? We need one more squeeze. Ready? Squeeze! Squeeze harder, harder, as hard as you can (pause about five seconds)! Great job! You did a great job squeezing these lemons to make a tasty lemonade. You can shake out your hand, wiggle your fingers if you would like to, and relax.*

*Now imagine you are a cute, little turtle basking in the summer sun. You are just resting on a rock by the pond enjoying the sunshine when uh oh! You feel danger! Quick little turtle! Tuck you head into your shell by lifting your shoulders up to your ears! Hide! Tighter! Tighter (pause about five seconds)! Oh phew! The danger went away. You are safe, little turtle - now you can just relax and enjoy the sunshine (wait for three seconds). Uh oh! Little turtle, you feel danger again! Quick! Hide in your shell! Tighter, tighter (pause about five seconds)! Okay, good. The danger has passed. You are safe now, little turtle. You can come out of your shell and just relax, enjoy the sunshine. Uh oh! Here comes danger one more time. Quick, little turtle, hide in your shell! Hold it! Tight, tighter… (pause about five seconds). Okay, you can relax. There is no more danger, and you are safe little turtle. Just relax and enjoy the sunshine.*

*Now I want you to imagine you are a cute, cuddly little kitten who is just waking up from a nap. What is the first thing a sleepy little kitten needs to do when they wake up? That's right, stretch. I want you to stretch your arms out in front of you as far as they will reach. Reach farther, farther (pause about five seconds). Good, you can relax your arms. Little sleepy kittens need more than one stretch, so this time, we are going to reach all the way up to the ceiling. Ready? Stretch! Higher, higher, as high as your arms will stretch (pause about five seconds). Good work! Okay, little sleepy kitten, this time we are going to do a rainbow stretch. I want you to reach your arms out in front of you as far as they will reach. Now lift them high above your head and reach all the way up to the sky. Stretch open your arms, like you are following the arc of a rainbow until you reach the ground. Doesn't it feel so good to stretch, little kitten?*

*This time, I want you to imagine you are lying in a beautiful meadow. There is a nice, warm breeze, the sun is shining, and it is a beautiful day. There are wild flowers growing and long grasses blowing in the wind. It is calm, peaceful, and very pretty. Suddenly, you notice that there is a baby elephant tromping around in the grass! He can't see us lying down in the meadow! Quick! You need to tighten your stomach by flexing your stomach muscles so it is like a rock! Hurry! Hold it tighter! Tighter (pause about five seconds)! Oh phew, he didn't step on us. We are safe. We can relax and enjoy this beautiful meadow. Uh oh! Here comes that baby elephant again. I think he might be lost and is looking for something. Quick! Make your stomach like a rock in case he steps on us! Hold it tight! Tighter, tighter (pause about five seconds). Great job, you can relax. We are safe, and he didn't step on us. You can just relax and enjoy this beautiful place. Oh no, here comes the baby elephant again. He is coming closer! Quick! Make your stomach like a rock; we don't want him to squish us! Hold it tight, tighter, and tighter (pause about five seconds)! You can relax now. The baby elephant found his mommy and is walking away with her. We are safe. Now, we can just enjoy this beautiful meadow.*

*Now, the best part of this meadow is the lake that is close by to it. And the best part of the lake is the mud! We get to squish our toes into the mud! I want you to imagine we are standing by this beautiful lake next to this beautiful meadow. Now we are going to squish our toes into the mud! Squish them down as far as you can go. If you are wearing shoes, you are going to squish your toes into the tops of them. Squish! Squish (pause about five seconds)! Now you can take your toes out, shake off the mud, and enjoy the beautiful lake. Only, it's too much fun to get into the mud just one time! So, let's squish our toes back into the mud. Can you feel the ooey, gooey, cold mud squishing through your toes? Squish them farther, farther (pause about five seconds). Great job. Let's take our toes out of the mud, give our feet a good shake, and relax. Now, we are going to squish our toes one more time. Squish them as deep as they will go! Squish! Squish (pause about five seconds)! Great work. We can take our toes out of the mud, shake them around, and really enjoy this beautiful lake now.*

*We have just one more place on our body that we need to stretch out. We are going to stretch out our face. I want you to imagine that there is a pesky little fly buzzing around and that it has landed right on your forehead! We are going to scrunch up our faces and wiggle them around to bump that pesky fly off (pause about five seconds). Phew! It flew away! Oh no! Here he comes again! This time, he has landed right on your nose! You need to wiggle up your nose, move it all around. Wiggle, wiggle (pause about five seconds). Get that pesky fly off! Phew! He flew away! Good job wiggling your nose! Oh dear! He has landed right between your eyes this time! Quick! Scrunch up your face! Wiggle your nose! Wiggle your eyes! Get that pesky fly away (pause about five seconds)! Oh good! He is going away for good this time! We can just relax and not worry about him buzzing around here anymore.*

*We have stretched out our bodies now from our heads to our toes!*

## PROCESSING QUESTIONS:

1. How does your body feel now?
2. What was your favorite stretch we learned?
3. Can you think of different situations where using the Lemon Squeezies can help you?
4. When can you use Lemon Squeezies in the future?

## CREATING A LEMON SQUEEZIE PUZZLE

A take-home prompt can help to remind the child to use their healthy coping skills, as well as offer a distraction from anxiety symptoms when putting the puzzle back together.

## DIRECTIONS:

On the blank puzzle, draw a picture of a lemon, turtle, kitten, elephant, mud puddle, and fly. It is helpful to draw these across the puzzle pieces, so when it is apart, there is some work to putting the puzzle back together.

The child can take this puzzle home and add it to his/her "toolbox" of healthy coping strategies.

# THE SUPERHERO IN
# THE MIRROR TECHNIQUE

Children who experience anxiety often feel helpless and overwhelmed. Helping the child to feel and believe that he/she can be empowered and take control of the worry is an important aspect of treating anxiety disorders. One of the ways to do this is employing the metaphor of a superhero and having the child list (with parents' and therapist support as needed) all of the traits a superhero possesses: strength, bravery, courage, etc. The child then dresses up as a superhero and thinks of all of the superhero powers needed to fight back against their anxiety symptoms. When they are ready, they can yell empowering messages such as "I'm not afraid of you, monster under my bed!" or "I am brave! I am strong! I can do this!" At the end of the session, you may want to either create or provide a superhero mask for the child to take home where they can practice being a superhero and saying their self-affirming and empowerment messages throughout the week. This intervention can be adapted for individual, family, or group therapy.

## SUPPLIES NEEDED:

> Superhero dress-up clothing (including masks, capes, shield, sword, magic wand, etc.)
> A full-length mirror
> Superhero mask or blank mask to give as a take-home "tool"

## DIRECTIONS:

1. Instruct the child to stand in front of the mirror in everyday clothes and describe the person seen.

2. Have the child choose one piece of dress-up clothing at a time. As the child begins to dress up, ask what superhero strength or super power each item represents. For example, a cape may represent super strength of being able to fly.

3. Continue having the child dress up, identifying different superhero powers the clothing represents. As soon as the child feels he/she looks like a superhero, have him/her describe the superhero seen in the mirror, as well as in their imagination.

4. Explore what it would feel like to be that superhero. Questions you may want to ask are:
   - What would you do if you were a superhero?
   - Who would you rescue or save?
   - What powers would you use to help others or yourself?

5. Have the child "practice" being this superhero and enact what could be done to change the situation the child is currently struggling with.

6. At the end of the session, write down the superhero powers the child already possesses and may not recognize. For example, "I am kind. I can use my muscles to help other people, like carrying a bag for my mom. I can stand up for my friends. I can say, 'Stop! I don't like this.'"

7. Instruct the child to do a "homework" assignment to practice being a superhero in the mirror every day.

8. As the facilitator, it can be helpful to give the child a superhero mask as a visual reminder to take home at the end of the session. If using a blank mask, invite the child to decorate it prior to ending the therapy session.

# WORRY CATCHER

I love the symbolism of a dream catcher and have one in my playroom. One day, a client said to me, "If we have a dream catcher to catch my bad dreams, can't we have a worry catcher to catch all of my worries?" That day, the worry catcher was born.

This play therapy intervention is modeled after the Native American symbol of a dream catcher. The traditional meaning of the dream catcher is to be a protector of sleeping people, especially children. The dream catcher was created to catch all the bad dreams and allow the good dreams to filter through to the sleeping child. The bad dreams were destroyed by the protection of the dream catcher. The worry catcher was created to help children identify, understand, and decrease the intensity of their worries. The child can determine which worries he/she is ready to let go of and which ones to keep.

## SUPPLIES NEEDED:

White board
Dry erase markers
Scotch Tape, markers, or pencils
Nerf™ Suction-Tipped Darts and Dart Gun
Paper squares
Envelope

**DIRECTIONS:**

**1.** Draw a big worry catcher on the whiteboard. You may want to draw one big circle, with smaller circles inside of it, drawing lines connecting the circles together. This may look similar to a Dream Catcher or any way the child would like it to look.

**2.** Write down as many worries as the child can think of onto separate paper squares.

**3.** Using a loop of scotch tape, tape one paper square to the end of the dart. Add one loop of tape to the outside facing piece of paper.

**4.** Load the dart into the dart gun and shoot it into the web. Shoot as many times as the child would like or as time allows.

**5.** All the worries that stick into the web are now "caught" by the worry catcher. Explore each worry with the child, rating its intensity on a scale of 1–10 (10 being the biggest, most worrisome and 1 being the smallest worry). With the child, discuss one coping skill the child can use to decrease the intensity of each worry. For example, the child who is afraid of the dark may keep a flashlight by their bed or spray "Monster Go Away Spray" (lavender essential oil) in their room before they are tucked in. Go through each worry on the web, rate it, and then brainstorm a coping skill that could be used to decrease or combat that particular worry.

**6.** For the papers that didn't stick into the web, the child can choose to reshoot towards the web or can choose to keep them or give to the therapist. Some children will want to put the worries into a worry box or special envelope to explore at a later date, or they may feel that they have given their worries away and are experiencing less distress.

**7.** It's important to note that not all children will be ready to explore each worry they write down during this activity. Make sure that you are giving the child permission to explore at his/her individual comfort level and ability. Each child will respond differently to this activity; some may only choose to explore one worry at a time, and you can use this as a check-in for future sessions with the worries that stuck in the web or as a part of ongoing treatment for anxiety-related disorders and feelings.

# MY VOLCANO INSIDE

Many children feel great big emotions inside and often act out or lash out in aggression towards others, as they lack the capacity for emotional language and, at times, healthy coping strategies. My Volcano Inside is an art-based play therapy activity that allows the child to give a visual representation of the emotions felt (and where they are felt) *before* a behavioral or emotional "explosion" take place. This can help the child to understand how their body gives them signals that their anger is about to explode and help them learn to manage their great big feelings in a healthy way.

## SUPPLIES NEEDED:

> Markers, crayons, paint, pencil
> Paper gingerbread body cut-out

## DIRECTIONS:

**1.** Explore how angry and worried feelings can build and build inside, much like a volcano with the hot lava building under pressure. Eventually there is so much pressure that the volcano explodes, spraying hot ash and lava all over the place. Our feelings can be like a volcano as well; when we bottle up our big feelings inside, eventually we "explode" and often leave an emotional yucky mess with the people and things we love.

**2.** Process with the client where they feel their "volcano" building inside of the body. You may ask questions such as:

- When you are mad, what does your belly feel like?

- When you start feeling mad, what does your heart feel like? Does it beat fast or slow?

- What do your fists or jaw feel like when you begin feeling angry?

**3.** Using any of the artistic tools available (crayons, markers, paint, etc.), instruct the child to draw on the cut-out what his/her volcano feels like, identifying where it resides in their body.

**4.** Explore what feelings feed the volcano inside. Identify and write down the different emotions and feelings the child experiences, taking notice if there is an association of color and feeling within the artwork.

**5.** Think of three ways the child can relieve the pressure inside of his/her volcano without exploding. An example could be, "I can talk to my mom when I feel mad inside" or "I can use my magic pinwheel and blow away my worry feelings."

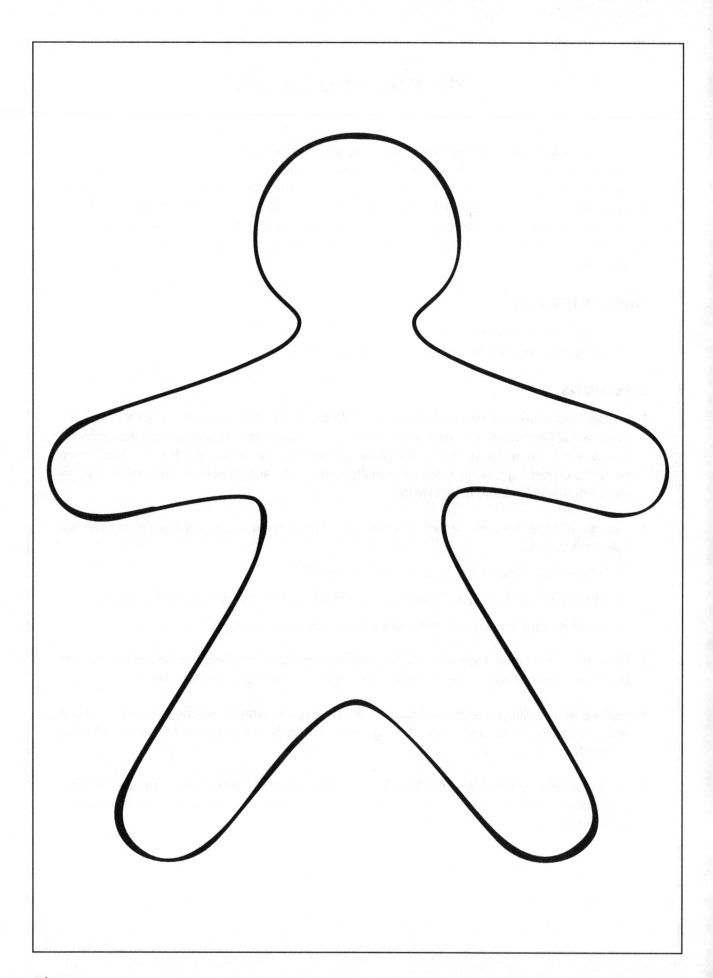

# Chapter 5 – Play Therapy Interventions for Autism Spectrum Disorder

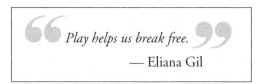

*Play helps us break free.*
— Eliana Gil

Autism Spectrum Disorder (ASD) is a *Diagnostic and Statistical Manual, 5th Edition*® (2014) (DSM-5®) diagnosis that is usually given after a thorough psychological evaluation, wherein the evaluator measures the child's or adolescent's behavior across a myriad of tests, assessments, and observations. ASD is a spectrum disorder, meaning the symptoms vary in intensity from severe to very mild. Common terms used to describe the variance include low and high functioning, or severe to mild impairment. Children and adolescents with ASD will likely have similar problem areas, but the severity of their difficulty and the presence or absence of other features (fine motor clumsiness, normal intelligence, increased or decreased verbal output) can vary (Coplan, 2010).

The Autism Society of America (2017) defines ASD as a complex developmental disability. Signs typically appear during early childhood and affect an individual's ability to communicate and interact with others. ASD is characterized by a certain set of behaviors and affects individuals differently and to varying degrees. Some of the behaviors associated with autism include delayed learning of language; difficulty making eye contact or holding a conversation; difficulty with executive functioning, which relates to reasoning and planning; narrow, intense interests; and poor motor skills and sensory sensitivities. Again, a person on the autism spectrum might exhibit many of these behaviors or just a few, or many others besides. The diagnosis of ASD is applied based on analysis of all behaviors and their severity.

There is no known single cause of autism, but increased awareness, early diagnosis, treatment intervention, and access to appropriate services and supports lead to significantly improved outcomes. Monteiro (2016) proposed that individuals with Autism Spectrum Disorder display a pattern of differences in their development, or style, that affects the way they use language and communicate with others; how they understand and participate in social relationships; the way in which they understand, manage, and regulate emotions; and how they respond to and manage sensory input and preferred areas of interest. ASD can affect a child in a myriad of ways with social, emotional, motor, developmental, and learning deficits all being present. For therapists working with children with ASD, it is essential to provide accurate assessment and evaluation in order to understand the level of impairment and equally understand the existing skill strengths of the child.

ASD ranges from severe to mild in terms of impairment of an individual. A child on the severe end of the spectrum may be unable to speak and have more serious developmental delays. A child on the mild end of the spectrum may be able to function in a regular classroom at school and eventually reach a point where he or she no longer meets the criteria for ASD. Even if two children have the same diagnosis, no two children with an ASD are alike. One child with an ASD diagnosis may be nonverbal and have a low IQ, while another child with the same diagnosis may have an above average IQ, and yet a third child may be verbally and intellectually precocious. Moreover, often the terms "low functioning" and "high functioning" are merely used to describe the child's placement on the autism spectrum (Exkorn, 2005).

A more accurate way to view the autism spectrum might be to view and assess each child individually, plotting where the child currently places in each developmental skill area. Because, in fact, children and adolescents with ASD do not fall into one of two categories – low or high functioning – each child has their own place on the spectrum according to their individual functioning and skill level (Grant, 2016a). Because of the range of manifestation and the myriad of issues that can accompany ASD diagnosis, it is essential that any treatment approach considers the individual child and aligns treatment to address the child's particular skill needs and issues.

## PARENT INVOLVEMENT

Parents and siblings affected by ASD are as much in need and deserving of the benefits of play therapy as any neurotypical client. In fact, play therapy approaches hold the possibility of not only individual therapy for the child with autism, but family therapy (including parent training) and specialized group therapy to address social and peer struggles. Play therapy techniques can represent a wide variety of interventions and be tailored to address the specific skill deficits that children and adolescents with ASD struggle with.

**Parents play a crucial role in their child's therapy**. Grant (2016b) stated that, as with any therapeutic approach, it is essential that relationship building be a central focus. Therapists should spend time in the beginning of and throughout treatment building relationships with children and adolescents and the parents they are working with. It is common for there to be a strained parent-child relationship when a child first enters counseling, as the parent can often feel alone and inept at parenting the challenging behaviors that can arise with ASD.

Many studies have examined the characteristics that create strong, healthy families, and most of these studies have indicated (among other characteristics) a healthy parent-child relationship and families having regular opportunities to spend fun time together as critical components for healthy families (Krysan, Moore, & Zill, 2010). Families that are experiencing an unhealthy system can benefit from participating in therapy that incorporates the whole family. This is especially true when one or more children are affected by ASD.

The process of family therapy and the inclusion of children in the family therapy process has existed in various forms for decades (Gil, 2015). In play therapy, theorists have identified the importance of including parent and child together in the family play process to address a variety of issues including ASD (Grant, 2015). Multiple family play therapy treatments exist that have had success in working with families affected by ASD, including Filial Therapy (VanFleet, 2014), Theraplay (Booth & Jernberg, 2010), and AutPlay Therapy (Grant, 2016a).

Gil (2015) expressed that play in family therapy can help individual family members shift rigid perceptions of each other. Through participating with their child in therapeutic play, parents are able to meet their child in his/her world and strengthen emotional connections, alter negative patterns of interaction and communication, and strengthen attachment bonds. Family Bubble Tag is a structured family play therapy intervention designed for children with ASD to bring the whole family together to increase relationship and social interaction skills, improve the parent-child relationship, strengthen attachment bonds, and create and model an atmosphere of the family experiencing fun time together.

# Case Study — Gavin

Gavin was five years old when he entered therapy with his biological mother. He had previously been diagnosed with Autism Spectrum Disorder and Attention Deficit Hyperactivity Disorder. Gavin lived with his mother and younger brother and had periodic visits with his biological father. His mother reported that Gavin was struggling in school and at home with behavior problems and seemed to be lacking appropriate peer social skills. She described Gavin's behavior problems as not listening (to teachers or to her); doing what he wanted; not following established rules; not interacting with peers; and lacking in cooperation, sharing, and joint play ability with peers. She also reported that Gavin had difficulties maintaining focus and seemed at times to be oppositional and defiant. Gavin's mother was hopeful that play therapy would help Gavin improve his behavior problems at home and school, increase his social skills, and improve his attention and focus ability.

Initial play therapy sessions were designed to build rapport and increase relationship development between Gavin, his mother, and the therapist. Beginning sessions also focused on assessment procedures, including therapist observations and having Gavin's mother complete parent self-report inventories. Assessment procedures resulted in establishing treatment goals to work on improved social functioning with peers and decreasing behavior problems, which were identified by the therapist as dysregulation episodes. The therapist and mother established that Gavin would participate in weekly sessions and initially focus on three primary treatment goals: increase in peer interaction-specific social skills, decrease in dysregulation (unwanted behaviors), and increase in attention and focus. The therapist would implement **AutPlay Therapy** (a family play therapy approach that incorporates play therapy methods and behavioral methods and is designed for children with ASD and other neurodevelopmental disorders).

Gavin's mother participated in all sessions with Gavin and the therapist. Therapy sessions were conducted in a typical play therapy room with additional sensory-focused toys such as a punching bag, exercise ball, Thera putty, water bead tray, and mini-trampoline. The therapist began by allowing Gavin to lead the play process and choose to play with or participate in whatever he liked. The therapist and Gavin's mother would join Gavin in his play, trying to allow Gavin the opportunity to work on turn taking and reciprocal play (mimicking typical peer play skills). The beginning sessions explored peer social skills to a minimal degree, and the therapist was careful not to push Gavin into a skill level that was beyond his ability. With each session, the therapist and Gavin's mother would try to increase Gavin's exposure to and his ability to engage in more appropriate peer-related interactions and play skills. Gavin's skill ability did increase as sessions progressed. After approximately 10 sessions, Gavin was participating in turn taking without becoming defiant and interacting in play with both the therapist and his mother without anxiety or resistance.

Around session 11, the therapist and Gavin's mother begin to implement a more structured approach to the sessions. The three would take turns picking a game or toy that they would all play with together. Each person's chosen play time would last about five minutes, then the next person would get to choose. This process continued until session 25. In the beginning, Gavin struggled when others got to choose what to play, and he routinely displayed resistance. Also, in the beginning, the time increments for each person's turn was five minutes or less, as that was approximately the amount of time Gavin could participate in another person's chosen play. When it was the therapist's or Gavin's mother's turn to choose a game or type of play, they would choose a more structured play intervention designed to increase peer social skills, regulation ability, and focus and attention. Throughout each session, the therapist was mindful of Gavin's dysregulation issues and monitored to ensure that Gavin was not challenged to the point of becoming too dysregulated and having a behavioral meltdown. Some sessions progressed more smoothly than others; this was considered part of the process for Gavin. Throughout the course of treatment, Gavin's mother was also implementing the turn taking and structured play interventions at home with Gavin. This provided Gavin the opportunity to work on treatment goals more often and to more quickly develop in his initially-identified skill deficit areas.

At session 25, Gavin was re-assessed with therapist observations and parent self-report inventories to identify treatment goal gains; he had shown improvement in all treatment goals. By session 25, he was participating with the therapist and his mother in taking turns, choosing games and play, and actively playing with the therapist and his mother in all the interventions and play without resistance. Gavin was also showing a better focus and maintaining his attention longer. Gavin's mother reported that behavior problems had decreased both at home and school. Gavin appeared to be calmer and less dysregulated. The school reported that Gavin was interacting with peers and school staff better. He was playing more with the other children and complying with teacher requests at a higher response rate than prior to beginning the AutPlay Therapy sessions. Gavin's mother and the therapist identified additional goals to address with therapy. Gavin kept participating in weekly sessions, and the therapist continued to implement structured play interventions designed to address treatment goals; she also taught the interventions to Gavin's mother, who would implement them at home.

## PLAY THERAPY AND AUTISM SPECTRUM DISORDER

Play therapy approaches hold many benefits for children and adolescents with ASD, especially in treating social and emotional issues they often experience. Play therapy is uniquely designed for and responsive to the individual and developmental needs of each child. Recently, there has been an increase in child therapy literature emphasizing play as the ideal way to treat social and emotional difficulties in children (Bratton, Ray, Rhine, & Jones, 2005; Josefi & Ryan, 2004). Research has shown that children diagnosed with ASD who participated in play therapy gained significant improvement in pretend play, attachment, social interaction, self-regulation, coping with changes, emotional response, and autonomy (Josefi & Ryan, 2004).

Rubin (2012) stated that several studies have shown benefits of utilizing the play therapy approach for children with ASD, including integrative models, child-centered play therapy, metaphor play, cognitive-behavioral play therapy, games, and LEGO play to improve social and affective functioning, reduce behavior problems, reduce anxiety, and improve emotional regulation ability. Grant (2016a) reported that family play therapy approaches, such as Theraplay® (Booth & Jernberg, 2010), Filial Therapy (VanFleet, 2014) and AutPlay® Therapy (Grant, 2016a), demonstrate success with children and their families affected by ASD. AutPlay Therapy mirrors working with families in ways that match established autism treatments and incorporates a play therapy base (including structured play therapy interventions) that is naturally engaging to the child with ASD.

Play therapy and play-based treatments can be appropriate interventions in working with children with ASD, especially when working with children who have little in the way of social skills and poor communication (Parker & O'Brien, 2011). Emerging research shows that play-based interventions are gaining more and more validity as effective treatment approaches for children and adolescents with ASD and other neurodevelopmental disorders. Play-based interventions provide the opportunity for the practitioner to individualize treatment and engage the child in a playful and natural way that other ASD treatments may not offer.

Grant (2016a) stated that working with children with ASD in play therapy requires some additional understanding and modification to the typical play therapy process. He proposed the following guidelines when implementing structured play therapy interventions with children and adolescents with ASD:

1. Develop a normal routine that the child or adolescent follows when entering the office or playroom to begin a session. Try to keep things the same from session to session. Children with ASD will respond more positively to things being predictable.

2. Some children and adolescents with ASD may have strong sensory issues. Practitioners should assess for these needs and adjust their office accordingly. This might include adjusting the lighting and noise levels, being flexible in where the child wants to sit, or eliminating certain odors, such as a scented candle.

3. When introducing a directive play therapy technique, break down the instructions into simple, understandable steps. If the child or adolescent is struggling to understand or complete an intervention, the practitioner may want to try completing one step at a time before giving the next instruction.

4. If necessary, model for the child or adolescent what you want him/her to do or create. Sometimes children need a visual representation of what is being asked of them. Children with ASD typically struggle with receptive language ability, so many children with ASD may struggle to understand intervention instructions if only given verbally.

5. Be prepared to participate in the play technique with the child or adolescent. Often the practitioner will be actively participating in helping the child, playing with the child, or creating his or her own representation of the intervention.

6. Give the child or adolescent feedback during and after techniques to encourage and praise them for how they did and what they accomplished, especially when the child or adolescent shows skill acquisition.

7. Be an observer during the session/technique to assess if the technique seems to fit the child or adolescent well and is appropriate for helping to reach established treatment goals. Notice if the child or adolescent is struggling, and try to assess how to help.

8. Ask the child or adolescent questions about the technique. Ask the child or adolescent if he/she enjoyed the technique or learned anything from the technique. Try to process the technique with the child or adolescent and apply the technique to real life.

9. Spend some time after the session to evaluate how the session went and if the technique seems to have been successful for the child or adolescent.

10. Fun is more important than form. Children and adolescents should feel safe, comfortable, and have fun during interventions. Keep in mind that children with ASD will likely experience some level of anxiety or dysregulation when addressing skill deficits.

11. A difficult to measure and often undervalued skill is the practitioner's playful instinct and attitude. Because many techniques involve addressing skill deficits and some techniques lack a great deal of enticement, the practitioner's playful attitude is essential for making the child's or adolescent's experience more engaging and enjoyable.

**It is the relationship with the child and family that makes the techniques work best!** There are countless examples of children who struggled with professionals simply because the therapy process wasn't focused on the relationship, but then later went on to reach great success and skill development with practitioners who *did* focus on the therapist-child connection.

Some children with ASD may not be able to participate in structured play therapy interventions due to a lack of attunement and engagement skills, as these techniques are more appropriate for children and adolescents on the autism spectrum who can engage with the therapist in at least some basic direction and reciprocal interaction. It may be possible to adjust a play therapy intervention to make it less involved and thus implement the intervention with a range of children, from those with a more severe impairment to those with less impairment. This should be scrutinized by the therapist, making sure the therapist has a solid awareness of the child's skill and functioning levels and that the play therapy interventions selected are a good match for the child.

Regardless of the play therapy intervention being used, the practitioner-child relationship is central to the child's realization of treatment goals. The rapport that develops between the therapist and child forms the foundation for therapeutic success. In building a therapeutic alliance, the therapist must create an atmosphere of safety in which the child is made to feel accepted, understood, and respected (Lowenstein, 1999). Play therapy interventions lend themselves to creating a very structured and directive session with a child or adolescent. The directive element of play-based interventions should never displace the importance for the therapist and the child to develop good rapport and a strong relationship.

Play therapy approaches have been successfully implemented for children, adolescents, adults, families, couples, and groups. Play therapy offers the ability to communicate inner processes and emotions without using verbal communication and can provide awareness properties to help put words to otherwise unidentified issues. The freedom from judgment and the ability to create and explore through play therapy offers safety for clients and facilitates through an almost innate desire that exists in all people – the desire to play.

# FAMILY BUBBLE TAG

This intervention helps children and adolescents with ASD improve in attachment with others, increase social skill development, improve relationship development with family, and assist in positive outcomes in parent-child relationships.

**SUPPLIES NEEDED:**

A bottle of bubbles for each member
A moderate to large space

**DIRECTIONS:**

1. Instruct the family that they will be playing a game of tag using bubbles. One family member is selected to be the person trying to tag the other family members (the first person selected to be the tagger should not be the child with autism).

2. Give the selected person a bottle of bubbles. When you say "go," the tagger must try to tag other family members by blowing bubbles and touching the other family members with bubbles.

3. The tagger can chase the other family members, and the other family members can try to move away from the tagger. Once a family member has been touched by any of the bubbles, that family member joins the tagger and is also given a bottle of bubbles. Now there are two family members working together to try and tag the rest of the family members with bubbles.

4. When a family member has been touched by bubbles, that family member joins the taggers until all family members have been tagged by the bubbles.

5. At the end of this intervention, all the family members will have been tagged, and each family member will have their own bottle of bubbles. At this point, instruct all the family members to blow their bubbles simultaneously and keep blowing as many bubbles as they can for one minute.

6. This intervention can be repeated with different family members beginning as the tagger.

7. Once the intervention has been played a few times, ask the family to sit on the floor in a circle and address some processing questions. This intervention can easily be adapted to be implemented in social skill groups with children and adolescents with ASD.

## PROCESSING QUESTIONS:

1. How did it feel to play this game with your family?

2. What did you notice about your other family members?

3. Did anyone seem reluctant to participate?

4. Did you think this was a fun time together?

5. Were there any problems or issues during the game?

6. What do you think was the most fun part of playing this game?

7. Which of your family members do you think enjoyed this game the most?

8. Was there any part of playing this game with your family that did not feel good to you?

9. Would you like to play this game again with your family?

10. Can you think of some other games you could play with your family?

**INTERVENTION PROCESSING:** Any person in the family can answer the processing questions, or the therapist might direct certain questions to specific family members. The therapist may also want to share observations and pay close attention to the family's process in completing the intervention and addressing processing questions. Gil (2015) noted that when facilitating family play interventions, both process and content should be carefully observed. Process observations refer to how the family communicates and interacts with each other, while content observations refer to what is talked about, what is suggested, and what is created.

Created by Robert Jason Grant, Ed.D, RPT-S

# BEACH BALL PLAY

Beach Ball Play provides an engaging and fun way for children and adolescents to work on a variety of developmental skills. It is also an easy intervention for children and adolescents to take home and play with other family members. This intervention involves three different beach balls, each with a focus on a specific area of skill development: emotional regulation, social skills, and coping skills. [Grant (2016b) proposed that children and adolescents with ASD often struggle in these three primary skill development areas.]

Fraser (2011) stated that in order for children with autism to decrease inappropriate and unwanted behaviors, they must increase their adaptive coping strategies. Beach Ball Play provides the therapist with a versatile structured play intervention that addresses coping skills and a range of skill deficits that are typical struggle areas for children with ASD. (This intervention is adapted from Robert Jason Grant's technique "Feelings Beach Ball" found in *Play-Based Interventions for Autism Spectrum Disorder and Other Developmental Disabilities.*)

Beach Ball Play is three interventions within the same concept. Goals include improvement in deficits typically found in children and adolescents with ASD; and improvement in emotion identification and expression, social skill development, engagement and reciprocal play skills, and coping and regulation ability.

## SUPPLIES NEEDED:

A beach ball and black sharpie pen

## BEACH BALL PLAY FOR FEELINGS

1. Blow up a beach ball and instruct the child that together, you and he/she are going to write feeling words all over the ball (you could also create a beach ball and write feelings on it prior to the child's session).

2. The child should think of as many feelings as possible, and then you can add feelings to fill up the beach ball. You will want to make sure that all feelings that the child needs to address are included. Some common feelings to include on the beach ball include anger, happiness, excitement, worry, nervousness, fear, love, calmness, peace, anxiety, sadness, embarrassment, shyness, loneliness, pride, and boredom.

3. Once the ball is complete, toss the ball back and forth with the child. When someone catches the ball, whichever feeling is closest to that person's right thumb is the feeling selected and the person must share what makes him/her feel that way; the other person then tries to guess what that feeling is (if someone's thumb lands on a feeling that has already been done, then the person should choose another feeling on the ball that has not yet been done).

4. An additional fun element would be to select different ways to toss the beach ball as it is passed back and forth, such as saying, "This time, let's hit it to each other with our heads!"

## BEACH BALL PLAY FOR SOCIAL SKILL DEVELOPMENT

1. Blow up a beach ball and instruct the child that they are going to write different ways to practice social skills all over the ball. (You could also create a beach ball and write social skills on it prior to the child's session.)

2. The child should think of as many social skills as possible, and then you can add social skills to complete the beach ball. You will want to make sure that all social skills that the child needs to address are included. Some common social skills include giving someone a compliment, looking in each other's eyes for 10 seconds, introducing yourself to someone else, saying "please" and "thank you," asking someone a question, practicing taking turns, speaking in an appropriate tone of voice, telling someone how you feel, demonstrating appropriate body language, and doing something kind for someone else.

3. Once the ball is complete, toss the ball back and forth with the child. When someone catches the ball, whichever social skill is closest to the person's right thumb is the social skill that the person must select and practice, typically through a role play with the other person. (If someone's thumb lands on a social skill that has already been done, then the person should choose another social skill on the ball that has not yet been done.)

4. An additional fun element would be to select different ways to toss the beach ball as it is passed back and forth, such as saying, "This time, let's hit it to each other with our thumbs!"

## BEACH BALL PLAY FOR COPING SKILLS

1. Blow up a beach ball and instruct the child that they are going to write coping skills all over the ball. (You could also create a beach ball and write coping skills on it prior to the child's session.)

2. The child should think of as many coping skills as possible, and then you can add coping skills to complete the beach ball. You will want to make sure that all coping skills that the child needs to address are included. Some common coping skills include taking deep breaths, doing jumping jacks, bouncing on an exercise ball, squishing play-dough, doing a yoga pose, stretching, coloring a mandala page, blowing bubbles, throwing a weighted ball, and hitting a punching bag.

3. Once the ball is complete, toss the ball back and forth with the child. When someone catches the ball, whichever coping skill is closest to the person's right thumb is the coping skill that the person has to demonstrate or practice. (If someone's thumb lands on a coping skill that has already been done, then the person should choose another coping skill on the ball that has not yet been done.)

4. An additional fun element would be to select different ways to toss the beach ball as it is passed back and forth, such as saying, "This time, let's hit it to each other with our knees!"

## PROCESSING QUESTIONS:

1. What social skills do you believe you are good at?

2. What social skills do you need to improve?

3. Why are social skills important?

**4.** Who is someone you know who has a lot of social skills?

**5.** Can you name 10 feelings?

**6.** Why do you think it's hard to talk about what you are feeling?

**7.** What is the best feeling?

**8.** What is your favorite thing to do that feels calm and relaxing to you?

**9.** What do you think feeling peaceful means?

**10.** Do you think it is ever normal to feel nervous?

**INTERVENTION PROCESSING:** This technique helps children and adolescents work on improving emotional regulation, increasing social skills, and developing coping and regulation tools. The therapist should focus on one area (beach ball) per session. One beach ball play will likely require a full session time. This intervention provides the therapist with three different interventions focusing on three different skill areas through the same concept. Therapists should consider which type of beach ball play should be implemented with the client or if all three would be appropriate. The therapist should pay close attention to areas the child struggles with and continue to implement this intervention in future sessions, focusing on the skill areas that seem to be the largest deficits for that child. If it is acceptable to the therapist, the child can take home the beach balls that are created and play the intervention with his/her family. This intervention can easily be implemented as a family play therapy intervention involving the whole family and as a group therapy activity. When implementing it as a group therapy intervention, the group can be divided into pairs using multiple beach balls or play with one beach ball as a whole group. The therapist should discern the best approach based on the comfort level and social interaction ability of the group members.

Created by Robert Jason Grant, Ed.D, RPT-S

# SOCIAL SKILLS BRACELET

Dawson, McPartland, & Ozonoff (2002) stated that children and adolescents with ASD tend to have a very limited concept of friendship, often face peer rejection, and may struggle with initiating socially-encouraging body language. Children and adolescents with ASD typically do desire to have friendships and interact with peers, but simply lack the social ability and skills to interact successfully. Thus, most attempts at some type of interaction usually are met with rejection and anxiety for the child with ASD. Repeated attempts to engage with peers only to be met with rejection can lead to what others may perceive as a lack of interest in connecting with peers (Grant, 2016a). Participating in play interventions such as Social Skills Bracelet can help children and adolescents learn social friendship skills to interact more successfully with peers and participate more fully in group and peer play.

Children and adolescents who participate in the Social Skills Bracelet intervention are expected to improve their friendship-related social skills. Children and adolescents with social skills struggles, especially related to friendship skills, will be able to practice connecting to peers; learning about and focusing on others; sharing in a natural, fun experience with peers; and practicing remembering names.

## SUPPLIES NEEDED:

Several different colors of yarn or string
Scissors

## DIRECTIONS:

1. Provide several different colors of yarn or string.

2. Have each participant go one at a time and choose the color of yarn or string that will represent that person. Each participant in the group must choose a different color.

3. After everyone has chosen, each participant shares with the group his/her name, something that he/she likes to do for fun, and why he/she chose the color of yarn or string.

4. Explain that the group is going to use the yarn to make friendship bracelets. Each participant in the group will be given a piece of yarn to represent each of the other participants in the group. For example, in a group of six, each participant will cut six pieces of yarn of the color chosen to represent themselves and give one piece of the yarn to each of the other five group members; thus, a group of six members will have six different colors of yarn or string to weave together.

5. Once each participant has all the other group members' colors, the group can then begin to construct their friendship bracelets.

6. Participants should be free to weave the yarn together in any manner they choose, but formal instructions for weaving the yarn together can be found at www.instructables.com/id/how-to-make-a-friendship-bracelet-1/ and on YouTube.

7. Once all the group members have completed their friendship bracelets, they should put their bracelets on their arms.

8. One at a time, each group member will talk about his/her bracelet by sharing information about each of the other group members who are represented in the bracelet. Each group member will share a color, the person who is represented by the color (saying the person's name), what that person shared that he/she likes to do for fun, and why that person chose this color to represent him/her.

9. If the participant who is sharing cannot remember something, the rest of the group can help him/her remember. It is likely that participants will not remember all information, such as names and why someone chose a particular color. This is a typical issue for children and adolescents with ASD.

10. Make sure that sharing times remain positive and that *not* remembering information is okay. You will want to clarify that all the group members are trying to remember, and that this is part of the process. Children and adolescents should not feel poorly about themselves if they cannot remember information.

11. The group will continue to share until each group member can successfully share each of the other members' names, what they said they liked to do for fun, and why they chose their color of yarn or string.

12. The participants should keep their bracelets and be encouraged to wear them at each group meeting, periodically trying to remember all the information about the other group members.

13. You can also encourage the participants to wear their bracelets throughout the week and periodically try to think about each of the other group members and remember information about them.

## PROCESSING QUESTIONS:

1. How does it feel to know that all the other children know your name and what you like to do for fun?
2. Is there anyone in the group who likes to do the same thing you like?
3. Why is it important to know and remember someone's name?
4. Why is it important to find out what other children like to do for fun?
5. Why is it important to share your name and things you like to do for fun?
6. Is there anything about this activity that made you feel uncomfortable?
7. How would you like to improve your friendship skills?
8. Why do you think it is sometimes hard to remember information about other people?
9. How does it feel to have no friends?
10. How does it feel if you have friends?

**INTERVENTION PROCESSING:** The therapist should take note of each participant's reaction to and participation in the intervention. The therapist will want to process with the group how the intervention felt to complete and also be sensitive to the anxiety and dysregulation that participants will likely experience while completing this activity. Part of the processing should include discussing how interacting and social engagement can create anxiety and dysregulation, and that this is to be expected when trying to work on developing these skills. Normalizing the uncomfortable feelings can help group members to participate despite the negative feelings they may be experiencing.

Created by Robert Jason Grant, Ed.D, RPT-S

# I Like it, I Don't Like it Puppets

This intervention works on helping children learn Theory of Mind, which is defined as the ability to understand that others can have beliefs, desires, and intentions that are different from our own (Grant, 2016a). Theory of Mind is often lacking in children with ASD, and this skill deficit can create significant emotional and social difficulties. Baron-Cohen (1995) stated that some people with ASD seem to lack all signs of Theory of Mind and coined the term "mindblindness" to represent this. Baron-Cohen (2000) further stated that most individuals with ASD possess some of the basics of Theory of Mind, but have difficulties in using it at a level that one would expect, given their intelligence in other areas. Theory of Mind deficits can range from severe through moderate, or even just very mild. Theory of Mind abilities can be expanded in children and adolescents with deficits through structured play-based interventions such as "I Like it, I Don't Like it Puppets." (This intervention is adapted from Robert Jason Grant's intervention "Theory of Mind (Tom) Puppets" found in *AutPlay Therapy for Children and Adolescents on the Autism Spectrum: A Behavioral Play-Based Approach*.)

**SUPPLIES NEEDED:**

A variety of puppets

**DIRECTIONS:**

1. Present several different puppets to be used in the intervention.

2. Explain to the child that they will be using the puppets to talk about how different people can have different thoughts and feelings about the same thing.

3. This technique uses puppets to help teach a Theory of Mind process to children, but miniature dolls could also be used if puppets are not available.

4. Begin by choosing three puppets (people puppets are preferable) and performing a simple story. Each puppet in the story has a different thought and feeling about the same thing. For example, each puppet tastes an apple pie; one puppet loves it, one puppet hates it, and one puppet says the pie is okay. Then the puppets taste a different kind of pie, such as a chocolate, and again, each one expresses a different thought and feeling about liking or disliking the pie.

5. The story should present three to four different examples of Theory of Mind.

6. Then repeat the puppet show and try to get the child to choose another puppet and participate in the story by pretending to taste a pie and giving his/her thoughts and feelings.

7. If the child is successfully participating, then try to get the child to create his/her own puppet story.

8. You can practice this intervention several times, implementing different stories all with the same theme of each puppet having a unique perspective.

9. You can also discuss the concept of Theory of Mind with the child after each puppet story.

10. The puppet stories should be animated and fun, and you should look for opportunities to get the child more involved in the story until the child can perform his/her own Theory of Mind puppet show.

## PROCESSING QUESTIONS:

1. Which puppet in the story do you think was right?

2. Why did the puppets have different thoughts and feelings?

3. Is it okay to think or feel differently than other kids about something?

4. What would happen if you liked a video game and your friend did not like it?

5. Have you ever liked a food that someone else did not like?

6. Do you know what it means to have a different opinion?

7. Can you think of an example of people having different opinions?

8. Let's try to think of something that you and I have different opinions about.

9. How does it feel to you when someone has a different thought or feeling from yours?

10. Can you create a puppet story with the puppets having different thoughts and feelings?

**INTERVENTION PROCESSING:** Moor (2008) stated that children with autism struggle with Theory of Mind, especially with understanding the thoughts, feelings, and beliefs of others. This technique is structured specifically to help children increase their ability level as it relates to learning Theory of Mind (when a child can understand that other people can have different thoughts and feelings from him or her about the same thing). Several stories can be developed and implemented with puppets, making sure that each puppet in the stories expresses a different thought and feeling designed to better help the child understand Theory of Mind. The therapist should utilize the processing questions to help measure how much Theory of Mind ability the child possesses and to assess gains that the child appears to be making through participating in this intervention. Therapists should understand that this intervention will likely need to be repeated several times before a substantial improvement in Theory of Mind ability can be noted.

Created by Robert Jason Grant, Ed.D, RPT-S

# AIRPLANE MODE CHARADES

Airplane Mode Charades helps children and adolescents learn to better interact with peers in the context of a safe group environment. This intervention is expected to help children and adolescents with ASD improve reciprocal social interaction with peers, reduce anxiety related to social interactions, and improve group social skill processes. Moor (2008) stated that before children with ASD can attempt to understand the thoughts, intentions, and feelings of others, they first need to be aware that "others" exist. Laushey & Heflin (2000) suggested that impairments in social behavior are so fundamental to children with ASD that social deficits should be considered the defining feature of ASD. Structured play therapy interventions, such as Airplane Mode Charades, specifically target improvement in social interaction and functioning for children and adolescents with ASD. When children with ASD are provided a less anxiety-producing, less stimulating, safe environment to practice improving social skill deficits, they can make skill gains and become more comfortable in social interactions (Grant, 2016a).

**CATEGORY:** Group

**SUPPLIES NEEDED:**

Index cards and pencils

**DIRECTIONS:**

1. Explain that each participant must think of something that he/she likes to do that could be done with another person. It must be something that does not involve electronics (hence "airplane mode").

2. Each participant writes his/her activity on an index card, not showing it to any of the other participants.

3. Collect all the index cards and, one at a time, act out the activities that are written on each index card.

4. The group members try to guess what the activities are, and then try to guess who in the group wrote down the activity.

5. Once an activity has been guessed and the group member who wrote the activity has been identified, the person the activity belongs to has to talk about how he/she could participate in the activity with another person.

6. The participant should try to identify who they could do the activity with and when and where they could do the activity.

7. This process happens for each group member after their activity has been acted out and guessed.

8. If the group members are at a social functioning level to act out the activity written on the index cards, then this activity should be repeated at another group meeting with the group members acting out the activities (instead of yourself or other group facilitators).

9. This activity requires a level of social comfort that may need to be progressively acquired. Many children and adolescents with ASD who struggle with social skills will be uncomfortable acting out an activity in front of a group of peers. You should consider this a goal, and at some point try to have the group members act out the activities.

## PROCESSING QUESTIONS:

1. Was it challenging to think of an activity to do with another person?

2. What are some activities that you currently do with peers?

3. What is something positive and something negative about playing video games with peers?

4. How does it feel to you to be in a group of peers?

5. Is it ever okay to be nervous around other people?

6. How would you feel if you never had any people contact?

7. Do you think you can get better at interacting with peers?

8. What is one of the worst things you can do in a group of people?

9. What was the most uncomfortable part of completing this activity?

10. What do you feel like you learned from this activity?

**INTERVENTION PROCESSING:** The therapist should have a discussion with the group members about participating in preferred activities with other people and how this may be an easier way to begin interacting with peers. The therapist and group facilitators should be mindful of dysregulation levels of the group members and be sensitive to any members who may not be comfortable participating. Some members may participate in short intervals or need to progressively work on group participation skills as the group meets. The therapist should ask the group members if any of the other activities shared are something that they would also enjoy doing. Group members should be encouraged to connect outside of the group meeting and participate in the activities with each other.

Created by Robert Jason Grant, Ed.D, RPT-S

# Chapter 6 — Play Therapy Interventions for Disruptive Behavior Disorders

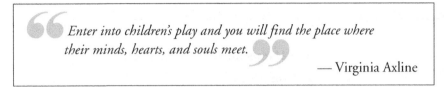

> *Enter into children's play and you will find the place where their minds, hearts, and souls meet.*
> — Virginia Axline

Childhood behavioral disruptive disorders consist of Oppositional Defiant Disorder (ODD) and Conduct Disorder (CD), which are the most common mental health diagnoses in childhood. Many clinicians view Disruptive Behavior Disorders (DBD) as a spectrum, with Oppositional Defiant Disorder on one end leading up to the more serious form of DBD, Conduct Disorder. Until the newest edition of the DSM-5®, Attention Deficit Hyperactivity Disorder (ADHD) was also included within this classification. Up to 50% of children and teens who have a diagnosis of ODD or CD also have a co-morbid diagnosis of ADHD (Gathright & Tyler, 2014). These different disruptive behavioral disorders impact the child greatly across different environments; their behavioral symptoms disrupt daily life in home, school, and community settings, as well as socially. The entire family system is affected due to the child's disruptive behaviors and actions, which may include:

- Ignoring rules
- "Goading" others
- Severe anger and rage outbursts
- Refusing to accept "no"

Within the diagnosis of DBD, symptoms are classified into three different criteria: angry/irritable mood, argumentative/defiant behavior, and vindictiveness. The nature of the behavioral symptoms helps the clinician to understand the child's struggles and give a correct diagnosis.

## OPPOSITIONAL DEFIANT DISORDER (ODD)

Kronenberger and Meyer (2001) define ODD as a "recurrent pattern of negativistic, disobedient, and hostile behavior directed towards authority figures" (p.83). Often, children who fit the diagnostic criteria for ODD possess certain characteristics that can be extremely challenging for their parents, teachers, and peers. These include:

- Arguing with authorities
- Refusal to comply with rules and requests
- Losing one's temper easily
- Irritability
- Blaming others instead of taking accountability
- Vengeful behavior
- Being annoying and provocative to peers and adults
- Often appearing to feel angry and resentful

Many children who are eventually diagnosed with ODD have early warning signs in their developmental history, as well as a family history of mental illness. Research has found that familial patterns of ODD are common in families in which at least one parent has a mental health history of depression, Oppositional Defiant Disorder, Conduct Disorder, ADHD, ASPD, or a substance abuse history (Gathright & Tyler, 2014). In homes with significant marital discord, ODD is also very common (Gathright & Tyler, 2014).

| Environmental Risk Factors | |
|---|---|
| | Parental rejection and/or neglect |
| | Harsh discipline |
| | Inconsistent parenting and/or multiple caregivers |
| | Lack of supervision |
| | Large family size |
| | Single parent status |
| | Marital discord |
| | Physical, sexual, emotional abuse |

| Common Risk Factors | |
|---|---|
| | **PARENTAL/FAMILY HISTORY OF:** |
| | Alcohol dependence |
| | Antisocial Personality Disorder |
| | ADHD |
| | Conduct Disorder |
| | Schizophrenia |
| | Sibling with DBD |
| | Maternal smoking during pregnancy |
| | Poverty |
| | Abuse and neglect |
| | Parental criminality and psychopathology |
| | Drug and alcohol use by parent/caregiver |
| | Exposure to violence |

An understanding of family dynamics is crucial to assess and treat a child in psychotherapy. Much of the behavioral dynamics that a child exhibits to warrant a diagnosis of ODD appear to stem from early chaotic relationships and negative parenting practices, as well as the exposure to prenatal substance use and violence. Many of these children have experienced broken or strained attachments with their primary caregivers, and while treating the behavioral symptoms is important, it is also crucial for the therapist to address the relationship dynamics as a whole and to view the repairing and healing of the parent-child relationship as the primary treatment goal. Working with the parents on more adaptive parenting strategies is also extremely important. Without addressing the attachment component of the problem, lasting change is unlikely to occur once treatment has ended.

## CONDUCT DISORDER

Conduct Disorder (CD) is a more severe diagnosis within the spectrum of Disruptive Behavior Disorders. There is a diagnosis of childhood onset as well as adolescent onset CD. Kronenberger and Meyer (2001) describe Conduct Disorder as "a repetitive and persistent pattern of behavior in which the basic rights of others or age-appropriate societal norms or rules are violated" (p. 86). When diagnosing CD, it is important to determine whether the symptoms began prior to or after age 10. A diagnosis of childhood onset CD requires at least one conduct problem to have begun before age 10. In this subgroup, the problem behaviors typically become more persistent. I remember clearly one of my teenage clients stating, "Any attention is better than no attention."

| CD Symptoms | |
|---|---|
| | Bullying |
| | Intimidating others |
| | Fighting (physical) |
| | Use of weapons |
| | Stealing (with and without confrontation of victim) |
| | Cruel behavior to animals and people |
| | Sexual coercion |
| | Lying |
| | Fire setting |
| | Running away |
| | Breaking into a house or car |
| | Truancy |

Many of the parents will need psychoeducation on the importance of a rewards-based parenting model (instead of the punitive model of parenting that is commonly established in these kinds of situations). A reward-based style means the parent "catches" the child being "good" by pointing out the positive actions and behaviors a child is engaging in, thereafter giving the child approval and positive attention. This helps to decrease the child's defensiveness, which increases the ability to recognize unhealthy behaviors and actions more quickly and allows the child to be willing to change. Garry Landreth has taught, "A child will change when they feel like they don't have to change," meaning that once children can feel accepted *as* they are, for *who* they are, there is room to make changes, and true therapeutic progress will commence (personal communication).

## PLAY THERAPY AND DBDs

Play therapy is an effective treatment modality to treat Disruptive Behavior Disorders due to its child-centered approach, which leaves the child as the "boss" or director of the play therapy session. When we can give the child a healthy sense of power in the therapy process, the maladaptive behaviors the child uses will decrease, as many of the negative behaviors a child exhibits are a means to create a sense of control, especially when the environment is completely outside of the child's control. Riviere (2009) emphasizes that children diagnosed with Disruptive Behavior Disorders need much more approval and unconditional positive regard from the clinician to help counterbalance the child's fear of incompetence and ultimately, rejection. Many of these children fear (and even expect) rejection from the adults in their lives; they may try to create a situation where their behaviors are so severe that they essentially become a self-fulfilling prophecy, which serves to reinforce their own belief that they are unlovable and unwanted.

Clinicians cannot overlook the importance of healing and repairing the child-parent relationship as an essential part of therapy. Teaching healthy social and emotional coping skills is important, but if the relationship dynamics in the home are not addressed, lasting change will be near impossible to achieve. Remember, a child's progress moves in tandem with the parents' progress, and a child alone cannot make lasting change in the family system.

The interventions chosen for this chapter can be utilized in individual, family, or group play therapy sessions and can be adapted to work with different ages and stages of development in clients.

# EXPLOSION!

Many children feel great big emotions inside, and often act out or lash out in aggression towards others, as they lack the capacity for emotional language and, at times, healthy coping strategies. Explosion is an art-based play therapy activity which allows the child to give a visual representation of the feelings felt (and where they are felt) *before* a behavioral or emotional "explosion."

This intervention is very similar to My Volcano Inside, as this intervention is used to teach the child to gain awareness of the somatic symptoms they may be experiencing in their bodies – such as racing heart, clenching jaw or fists, breathing quickly – prior to an emotional or behavioral outburst. The child is able to identify the emotions that accompany their somatic complaints and learn how to calm down their bodies before "exploding."

## SUPPLIES NEEDED:

Markers, crayons, paint, pencil
Blank paper
Glue

## DIRECTIONS:

**1.** Explore how angry and worried feelings can build and build inside, much like the bubbles inside a can of soda that gets shaken up. Eventually there is so much pressure that the soda can will explode, spraying sticky soda all over the place. When we bottle up our big feelings inside, we are like a shaken soda can as well. Eventually, we "explode" and often leave an emotional "sticky" mess with the people and things we love.

**2.** Draw or create a generic soda can on a large piece of paper. Instruct the child to identify specific situations and emotions that "shake their can" (e.g., feelings of frustration and distress) and draw them onto the soda can picture. They can also cut out pictures from magazines to represent their different experiences and glue them onto the soda can.

**3.** Explore what feelings and emotions "shake up" the can much like how it would feel if they were a can of soda. You may need to teach the child about how the carbonation inside of the soda can builds up significant pressure if the can is shaken up. Identify and write down the different emotions and feelings the child experiences on the soda can picture, taking notice if there is an association of color and feeling within the artwork.

**4.** Think of three ways the child can relieve the pressure inside of their soda can without exploding. An example could be, "I can talk to my mom when I feel mad inside" or "I can use big deep breathing and blow away my worry feelings." Write these next to the soda can.

# FEELING MONSTERS

Children often have big worries and concerns about their world. Depending on their chronological, as well as emotional, age, they may lack the necessary language to express *what* they are feeling or *how* they are feeling. Children may act out their worries with negative or undesirable behaviors including crying, whining, aggression, anger, shyness, school refusal, separation anxiety, and panic attacks.

The goal of this activity is to first create a visual, tangible object to represent their feelings, and second, to begin identifying what is "feeding" their worry, anger, etc. This intervention is very useful in family therapy as it helps to normalize feelings, even undesirable feelings, and helps decrease the scapegoating of the family problems onto the identified client. In family therapy, each member of the *family* will work on identifying their own individual emotions throughout the week rather than focusing on the behaviors of the child who is acting out.

## SUPPLIES NEEDED:

Empty facial tissue box
Paint, stickers, pipe cleaners, feathers, etc.
Washable paint
Glue
Scissors
Googly eyes
Spray paint
Egg carton (empty)
Emotions chart
Construction paper

**DIRECTIONS:**

**1.** Prior to the play therapy session, you may want to spray paint the entire tissue box to cover the branding and design. The child may have picked out what color the box should be. You can also paint the tissue box in session. The empty tissue box will become the main body of the monster.

**2.** Invite your client and their family to decorate the box to become a feeling monster, using any art supplies they choose. The monster box can be any feeling that the child and/or family chooses to focus on. Suggestions for art supplies you may want to offer: googly eyes, pipe cleaners, feathers, stickers, etc. The child may choose what feeling he/she needs help with, or the therapist may instruct what feeling (based on the presenting problem) the monster will be.

**3.** The mouth of the feeling monster is the opening where the tissues come out. You may want to make "teeth" out of construction paper and glue them to the inside of the opening.

**4.** Give the monster to the child and parent to take home with them at the end of the session. Throughout the week, instruct each member of the family to either draw a picture of what they are feeling or write down (if they are older) what is causing them to feel emotionally charged. For example, if the monster is an angry monster, the child may draw a picture of feeling mad when he is told "no."

**5.** For the next few sessions, instruct the parent and child to bring their monster to therapy with them. In session, empty the contents of the monster and explore together what the monster was "fed" throughout the week.

**6.** With the parents' involvement, identify with the child different healthy and/or positive ways the child can address big feelings and practice coping skills together.

# BULLSEYE

Bullseye is a fun, high energy play therapy technique developed to teach children emotional intelligence and to begin identifying different feelings and emotions. In this technique, a child is able to experience the "dance" of play therapy – great big play, quiet down to process, then back to great big play. A client can utilize big bursts of energy and movement, then learn to quiet down the body and process different questions. Once a child has answered the questions, they can go back to great big play again. This not only teaches the child awareness of emotions and feelings, but how to center and quiet their body and brain amid distractions and dysregulation.

The goal of this intervention is to help children: (1) understand the meaning of different emotions, (2) identify how different emotions feel inside the body, and (3) identify a time when each of the different emotions has been felt.

## SUPPLIES NEEDED:

Feelings chart (I use a large laminated poster size that is framed and has cartoonish characters)
Nerf gun
Suction tipped darts

## DIRECTIONS:

**1.** Instruct the child that the goal of this "game" is to try to aim and shoot the different faces on the feelings chart. The child will earn one point if able to shoot a "bullseye" onto one of the faces.

**2.** Once the child is able to get a "bullseye," the shooting stops momentarily. You will ask the child three questions:

- Do you know what this word means? (and explain the definition of the feeling)

- Where do you feel this feeling inside your body?

- When is the last time you felt this feeling?

**3.** The "big" play then resumes until the child is able to get another bullseye.

**4.** Continue this play until the child has hit all the different feelings on the chart.

**5.** Give the child a copy of the feelings chart to take home.

# MOSAIC FEELINGS BOWL

Get ready for a sticky, messy, wonderful play therapy intervention! This creative art-based intervention helps children and teens increase their understanding of verbal and nonverbal expressions of emotions and feelings. It also helps to increase coping skills of frustration tolerance, as the creative arts activity can become more challenging and requires the client to utilize problem-solving skills.

## SUPPLIES NEEDED:

Latex balloon
White glue
Scissors
Paint brush or sponge to spread glue
Tissue paper (Kleenex) or toilet paper
At least six different colors of construction paper
Mod Podge® (optional)
Jar or bucket to hold the balloon
Wet wipes, paper towels for cleaning hands
Tarp or plastic sheet to protect carpet (optional)

## DIRECTIONS:

## SESSION 1:

**1.** Ask the client to pick one balloon, blow it up, and tie it at the end. Place the balloon (with the smooth side up) inside the mouth/opening of a bucket or a jar so it's easier to work with.

2. Instruct the client to match a color to an emotion he/she feels. It is useful to provide different colors of construction paper and a feelings sheet in case the client struggles to identify feelings (tell the client to pick not only positive feelings, but difficult, painful ones as well). Allow for at least six colors/feelings. Once the client has matched colors to feelings, ask which three of the feelings/colors selected are the client's biggest struggle – the feelings kept deep inside, possibly even hidden from others.

3. Have the client cut the first three feelings/construction paper into small pieces (they can be any shape). As the client may get tired of or bored by cutting the paper, be prepared to assist in this process. Spread glue over the rounded surface of the balloon, then start pasting the first three feeling/colors of construction paper, adding as much glue as necessary to make sure all pieces of paper are covered.

4. Paste a layer of tissue or toilet paper over the first three colors, adding as much glue as necessary to cover the tissue paper.

5. Cut the last three feelings/colors into small pieces, spread more glue over the tissue paper if necessary, and add the three remaining colors of construction paper to form the outer layer.

6. Once all mosaic paper pieces are stuck to the balloon, add one more coat of glue or Mod Podge. Some clients like to add some leftover color pieces from the first feelings phase, which is okay! Allow the balloon to dry until the following session.

**SESSION 2:** The balloon will now be dry.

1. Instruct the client to pop the balloon. If the client is uncomfortable with the noise of a popping balloon, you can do this prior to the session. Once popped, there will be a mosaic paper bowl of feelings left.

2. Remove the balloon from the inside of the bowl. Children and teens are usually delighted to see their bowl creations!

3. Invite the client to explore these feelings in more detail now that he/she is "holding" them. You can bring to the client's attention the feelings that they keep deep inside versus the feelings they are able to display on the outside. If some of the inside feelings are also displayed on the outside of the bowl, you can ask questions such as:

   • When do these inner feelings come out?

   • How do you handle and/or recognize these feelings?

   • What coping skills can you use when you feel these different emotions?

4. The bowl can then be taken home and used by the client to store some self-soothing items in. These items may include play-dough, bubbles, fidgets, gum, smooth rocks, etc.

Created by Shirla Pamp, LMFT, RPT

# Chapter 7 – Play Therapy Interventions for Depression

> *" Play is child's work, and this is not a trivial pursuit. "*
> – Alfred Adler

Childhood depression is a well-known mental health issue that affects children throughout the different ages and stages of development. Research estimates vary, but it is recognized that up to 3% of elementary-age children and 8% of adolescents experience depression (Zhou et al., 2015). Zhou et al. (2015) reports that the average length of depression lasts about nine months, but a staggering 70% of children will experience a recurrent episode of depression within five years of their initial episode. Sadly, many children will experience depression into adulthood and throughout their lives. The World Health Organization has deemed depression to be the leading cause of disability and the fourth leading contributor to the global burden of disease (Anderson, Cesur, & Tekin, 2015). Due to these statistics and the long-term physical, emotional, and mental health consequences of depression, it is important for clinicians to treat this disorder effectively and not minimize or overlook the symptoms their young clients may be experiencing.

It is now well-documented that infants through preschool-age children can experience depression and that their symptomology is characteristic of depressive disorders (Kronenberger & Meyer, 2001). In infancy, depression typically is manifested in behavioral flatness and attachment disruption – this may be indicated through whining, withdrawal, stunted or regression in growth, weight loss, and dazed and immobile facial expression (Kronenberger & Meyer, 2001). Toddler depression affects children ages 1–2 years of age, and symptoms may include irritable mood and a delay in developmental milestones, including walking, standing, talking, and toilet training. Nightmares and night terrors are also common in this age group. Toddlers with depression may also engage in self-stimulating behaviors, such as rocking, masturbation, and head-banging (Kronenberger & Meyer, 2001). There is also often a decrease in play, as the toddler becomes more clingy, fearful, and anxious.

In preschool-age children (3–5 years old), depression often takes on a more affective and behavioral manifestation. Symptoms such as sadness, weight loss, motor retardation, lethargy, suicidal ideation, anger, illness, and apathy can be present (Kronenberger & Meyer, 2001). Depressed preschoolers experience anhedonia, changes in sleep, appetite, behavior, and activity level, as well as excessive guilt (Luby, 2010). They may be less likely to engage in play and are able to verbalize feelings of sadness, worthlessness, and fear.

School-age children (ages 6–12) and adolescents who experience depression begin to resemble adult symptoms in terms of cognitive, mood, behavioral, and physical symptoms. Children and teens may experience impaired social functioning and a high level of risk associated with self-harm ideation as well as suicidal behaviors (Zhou et al., 2015). This may create a self-fulfilling prophecy: The child believes him/herself to be worthless or not well-liked by peers, which increases the likelihood that the child will withdraw or engage in an impaired social manner. The resulting experiences of isolation and rejection then exacerbate the child's initial feelings of worthlessness and low self-esteem, and the vicious cycle of depression continues.

Depressed teens display a range of coexisting emotional and behavioral problems, and report higher levels of anxiety, inattention/hyperactivity, aggression, substance abuse, and PTSD (Jaycox et al., 2009). Adolescent depression has a considerable negative impact on school performance, including difficulties with concentration, social relationships, reading and writing, as well as cognitive distortions that homework and schoolwork is overwhelming and too difficult to engage in (Frojd et al., 2008). Research has also shown that adolescents who experience depression may be more inclined to act out and engage in property destruction and other impulsive crimes (Anderson et al., 2015). The risk of suicide also increases substantially in adolescents who experience depression. Adolescent depression is associated with a broad range of negative health issues, including suicide attempts, completed suicides, and negative health outcomes, such as pregnancy and early parenthood (Jaycox et al., 2015).

## Symptoms of Depression

| | |
|---|---|
| Difficulty concentrating | Weight gain or weight loss |
| Fatigue and decreased energy | Loss of interest in activities or hobbies once pleasurable |
| Feelings of guilt, worthlessness, and/or helplessness | Overeating or appetite loss |
| Feelings of hopelessness and/or pessimism | Anxiety or excessive worry |
| Crying spells | Persistent aches or pains, including stomachaches, headaches, and body aches |
| Social isolation | Persistent sad and anxious feelings |
| Insomnia, early waking, or excessive sleeping | Academic decline |
| Irritability/anger | Decline in personal hygiene and self-care behaviors |
| Oppositional behaviors | Thoughts of suicide or self-harm |
| Restlessness | Suicide attempts |

## FAMILY RISK FACTORS

Depression that develops in infancy or early childhood tends to be connected to poor family relationships and functioning, as well as environmental causes. Poor parental care, neglect, abuse, and family conflict have been shown to be significant contributors to the development of depression, as are parental mental health issues (Gledhill & Hodes, 2015). In infancy, depression typically develops in babies who are emotionally deprived and experience chronic separation from their primary attachment figure within the first year of life (Kronenberger & Meyer, 2001). These separations may be physical, such as when an infant is hospitalized, or emotional, as when the infant experiences extreme emotional unavailability from the primary attachment figure (Kronenberger & Meyer, 2001). A parent who experiences depression is likely to have a child who experiences depression, as there is a strong genetic predisposition, especially in adolescent-onset depression (Gledhill & Hodes, 2015; Kronenberger & Meyer, 2001).

Environmental influences, such as homelessness, are also significant risk factors for childhood depression. Research has shown that homeless children have higher rates of depression and anxiety (Baggerly, 2004). Parental substance abuse, poverty, and anti-social behaviors are also high-risk factors.

# Case Study — Daniel

Daniel is a 10-year-old boy who was referred to play therapy after his teacher informed his parents that he had been writing in his school journal that he had recently experienced thoughts of hurting himself and even that he wished he would die. Daniel's parents were shocked to learn that their child had been having suicidal thoughts. They had noticed he had seemed more withdrawn and "off" recently, but had not thought too much of these changes. His parents report that they had been highly stressed, as Daniel's father had recently lost his job and resulting health insurance. His mother reports she had been diagnosed with Major Depressive Disorder, PTSD, and Generalized Anxiety Disorder and had stopped taking her medication when the pills had run out, feeling that the family could not spare the additional expense of her medications.

In the initial intake, Daniel presented as withdrawn, apathetic, and disengaged. He came into the playroom and laid his head down on the table, would mumble answers to questions he was asked, and refused to engage with his play therapist. He eventually agreed to touch the sand in the sand tray with little enthusiasm. As Daniel began running his fingers through the sand, he appeared to relax and let down his guard slightly. Daniel began making mounds of sand in the sand tray and asked if he could get the sand wet so it would stay in the shape he was making. He was told he was the boss in the playroom and could do what he liked with the sand.

Daniel got a cup of water and began sprinkling it over the sand until it was the desired consistency. As he made the hills in the sand, he picked up a small piglet figurine from the shelves by the sand tray and buried it in the sand hill. He began looking at the shelves of figurines and found one of a woman who looked as though she was screaming. He placed that figurine in the sand and buried it in the hill as well. Next, Daniel took a figurine of a large ox and placed it on top of the sand hill. He then began pouring water over the figure, melting the sand and ox together. Throughout this play, Daniel did not speak a word. At the end of the session, Daniel looked up at his play therapist, briefly smiled, and said, "I feel a little bit better now." Daniel attended weekly play therapy for the next several weeks, each time returning to the sand tray and figurines.

Over time, Daniel's affect changed from flat and blunted to a healthy, expansive expression. He would walk into the playroom playfully but also with purpose. He began verbalizing his emotions and worries, learning how to ask for help from others, and using healthy coping skills. His parents were able to participate in the therapeutic process and learn healthier ways to engage with their child. They learned how to offer reassurance that they could hold his "big feelings" and express that his depression was not his fault, nor were the family financial difficulties.

## PARENT INVOLVEMENT

Due to the nature of the high likelihood of attachment injuries present in childhood depression, the parent-child relationship is once again a crucial aspect of treatment. It is beneficial to teach healthy coping strategies to both parent and child so they can work on these skills outside of therapy (provided there is enough emotional safety in their relationship to do so). If parents manifest high levels of depressive symptoms, it may be necessary to refer them to individual therapy prior to engaging in family play therapy. Research has demonstrated that including parents in the therapeutic process helps to alleviate the toxicity of the family environment, develop coping strategies, and improve the parent-child relationship (Diamond & Josephson, 2005). By helping families learn to resolve conflicts and rebuild trust with one another, the depressive symptoms of the child can be decreased (Diamond & Josephson, 2005). In addition, helping parents experiencing depressive symptoms learn healthy coping skills can alleviate the child's depression.

## PLAY THERAPY AND DEPRESSION

Play therapy offers the child and parent a safe, nurturing environment to learn new coping skills, communicate their emotions in a healthy manner, and improve their relationship. Research has shown that parent involvement dramatically improves the outcome of play therapy (Gil, 2015). Play therapy encompasses such a wide range of interventions and applications that it is possible to tailor it to the individual family's needs.

For example, one family may need extra support in learning how to validate one another's feelings and improve their emotional intelligence. They may need to learn skills in emotional intelligence and how to cope effectively with their big feelings. Utilizing a CBT approach may be very beneficial to help them develop these skills.

In another family, the parent's depression may be exacerbating the child's depression, and incorporating a child-centered play therapy approach may be very beneficial, as the child may have felt voiceless and invisible to the parent. Filial play therapy has been shown to be very successful in treating a wide range of psychosocial problems, including depression (Gil, 2015).

# HAPPY THOUGHT POT

The Happy Thought Pot is a creative arts intervention that is based on a CBT approach to play therapy. Often, when a child or teen is experiencing depressive symptoms, it is difficult to think beyond the emotional pain or to find hope that things will improve. The Happy Thought Pot helps the child to think about positive thoughts or to find little pieces of hope to hang onto during the week in between therapy sessions. Every day, the child will write down one more happy or hopeful thought and place it into the Happy Thought Pot, which eventually becomes the anchor point for the flowers to stand up straight, representing the child learning mastery over negative thoughts.

This intervention can be utilized in individual, group, or family therapy and is appropriate at all stages of the therapeutic process.

## SUPPLIES NEEDED:

Flower pot (any size)
Variety of pipe cleaners
Paper and writing utensils
Scissors
Markers or paint/paint brushes
Happy Thought Pot Worksheet (p.73)

**DIRECTIONS:**

1. Give each child or family member a plain flower pot. Instruct them to decorate the outside of their flower pot to represent happiness, joy, or hope. They may decorate their flower pot using markers or paint.

2. Once the pots are all decorated, allow the child to choose 4–6 pipe cleaners of various colors.

3. Instruct the child to choose one pipe cleaner that will be the flower head. Direct the child to wrap the pipe cleaner around a finger. This will look like a spring when it is complete.

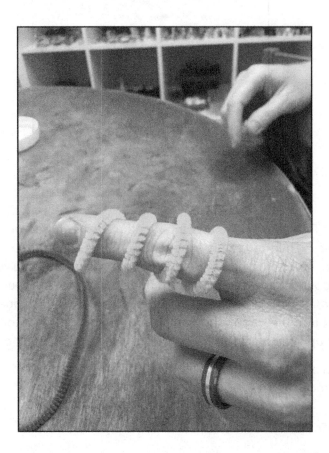

4. Instruct the child to choose another pipe cleaner that will become the stem of the flower. Fold the pipe cleaner in half, then on one side, fold it in half once more. Twist the ends together.

**5.** Push the straight end of the stem through the middle of the spring-shaped pipe cleaner. Twist the straight end of the stem to secure the pipe cleaners together. This should create a "flower."

**6.** Follow the instructions to create two or three additional pipe cleaner flowers.

**7.** Place the flowers into the pot. It is normal that the flowers will fall over, as there is nothing to support them to stand up.

**8.** You can then say something such as, *"Flowers need nourishment to grow and stand up. They need rain and sun, as well as healthy soil to grow in. Our positive thoughts are like the flowers; we need to provide a healthy place for them to grow and develop as well as proper nourishment to grow. We can "nourish" our happy or positive thoughts each day by taking time to remember them, write them down, share them with family members, and practice thinking about them. Each day as we do this, our positive and hopeful thoughts will grow stronger and stronger, just like flower seedlings when they are nourished by the sun and water."*

**9.** Instruct the child to cut the piece of paper into strips, one for each day of the week. Every day, the child is to fill out a Happy Thought paper strip and then fold it up and put it into the flower pot. Over the course of the week, if the child can write up Happy Thoughts each day, the flowers will continue to "grow" and eventually stand up straight because there will be enough happy thoughts to anchor them.

**10.** Each week, the child should bring back the Happy Thought Pot to explore what happy thoughts nourished the flowers during the week. You could also give the child a small potted flower or flower seeds to take home to help them remember how important it is to nourish the flowers to help them grow - just like the child's happy thoughts!

# HAPPY THOUGHT POT

**My happy thought today is:** _____

**My happy thought today is:** _____

**My happy thought today is:** _____

**My happy thought today is:** _____

**My happy thought today is:** _____

**My happy thought today is:** _____

**My happy thought today is:** _____

73

# COPING ON THE CUFF

In this intervention, the child creates a bracelet to wear daily as a reminder of the coping skills identified to combat depressive thinking and symptoms. Each bead on the bracelet is symbolic of a different skill or strategy that can help the child cope in a positive and healthy manner. This intervention is appropriate for both boys and girls, as children are allowed to be creative and choose the style of beads that best represents their individual sense of style and personality. When financially feasible, the therapist may choose to instruct the parent and child to go to a bead store and purchase the beads of their choice. This provides an opportunity for a fun outing and positive interaction between the parent and child. If this would be burdensome on the family, the therapist can provide a selection of different colored and shaped beads the child can choose from in session.

This intervention is most useful during the middle or working phases of treatment, after the child has begun learning new coping strategies and ways to manage depressive symptoms and negative thinking errors. It can be adapted to individual, group, or family therapy.

## SUPPLIES NEEDED:

Variety of beads
Stretchy bracelet cord
Scissors

## DIRECTIONS:

**1.** Provide the child with stretchy bracelet cord. Measure how much string would be needed to wrap around the child's wrist and cut the string accordingly. You may want to cut the string slightly longer than what is actually needed, as additional string is needed to knot the ends.

**2.** Allow the child to sift through the beads and choose one bead to represent each coping skill he/she has identified as useful. You may need to coach the child to help him/her remember the healthy coping skills recently learned and used. Some ideas of healthy coping skills are:

- Ask for a hug

- Take five deep breaths

- Remember my Happy Thoughts

- Take a walk

- Listen to uplifting and positive music

- Write in my journal

- Call a friend

- Find some way to give service to another person

**3.** It can be helpful to play quiet, soothing music while the client is looking at the beads and thinking of the coping skills. For older tweens and teens, an additional therapeutic strategy is to ask the teenage client to prepare a playlist of positive or soothing songs prior to session to listen to together while making the bracelet.

**4.** Instruct the child to begin stringing the bracelet to achieve the desired look. The child may use smaller beads in between the designated coping beads to allow for space and design as desired. The child directs the therapist how to be helpful in the process, such as by holding on to one end of the string, etc. If the child would rather do it independently, that is permissible and can be a good teaching moment in asking for help as well as in self-reliance and resiliency.

**5.** For each coping bead, process with the client how this bead represents the identified coping skill and what it means. Questions you may want to ask are:

- How does this bead represent the coping skill?

- When you look at this bead, what stands out and can help you remember the skill it is connected to?

- What can you do to use this coping skill? Ask the child to give an example of how to implement a coping skill to show understanding and mastery.

**6.** When the bracelet is complete, tie the ends into a secure knot (or an older client can do this). A square knot is typically most secure and easy to do.

**7.** The child can take the bracelet home and wear it daily to help them remember to use healthy coping skills.

# REVERSE FEELINGS CHARADES

Reverse Feelings Charades is a fun, dynamic group activity that turns the original game of Charades™ on its head! In this intervention, the group or family members work together to identify different feelings and strengthen their emotional intelligence skills by learning how to recognize different facial expressions, exploring where a person may feel the different emotions in their body, and how to identify when someone else is experiencing a certain emotion, thereby developing empathy skills as well. Get ready for lots of laughing as the intervention gets started. The group has to act out the different emotions, and the person who is "It" has a chance to name that feeling before time runs out!

**SUPPLIES NEEDED:**

Printable feeling cards (or magazines, cardstock index cards, glue)
Timer

**DIRECTIONS:**

**1.** Cut out the printed feeling cards and stack them into a pile.

**2.** If you are making your own cards, cut out different facial expressions from magazines and glue them onto the index cards. Identify the emotion expressed and write it beneath the picture.

**3.** Designate one person to be "It." You may want to choose oldest to youngest and move in that order.

**4.** The group chooses the first card in the pile and will act out that feeling to the person who is "It" without allowing that person to see the feeling card.

**5.** The person who is "It" stands in front of the group and has 60 seconds to determine what emotion the group is acting out.

**6.** If playing with a large group, you may want to split everyone into teams. Whenever a person "wins" by identifying the actual feeling, a point is earned for the team.

**HAPPY**

**SAD**

**MAD**

**WORRIED**

**EXCITED**

**CALM**

**FRUSTRATED**

**DEPRESSED**

**CONFIDENT**

**SCARED**

**SILLY**

**SURPRISED**

**CONFUSED**

**EMBARRASSED**

# SHOW ME YOUR HEART 3D

Show Me Your Heart 3D is an art therapy intervention and can be utilized in many different creative ways. I enjoy utilizing this in family, group, and individual therapy as a means of "checking in" with yourself and others – how you are feeling and what emotions you are holding inside of you. Creating an expressive arts project can be a powerful experience and give language to your feelings when it has been difficult to find words to articulate what it feels like emotionally. There are many different versions of this expressive arts therapy technique, and the original author is unknown.

## SUPPLIES NEEDED:

Plain paper
Crayons, markers, colored pencils
Glue
Scissors
Various tactile objects: buttons, natural elements, feathers, paper scraps, etc.

## DIRECTIONS:

**1.** Instruct the child to draw a heart big enough to fill the entire paper (8½ × 11 inches).

**2.** The child can choose which art supplies they would like to use to fill up their heart. The child can choose as many colors and feelings as desired. Instruct the client to fill up the entire heart with colors, representing the "amount" of emotions felt.

**3.** The child can then glue on extra materials using craft supplies and/or small objects (such as buttons or feathers) to represent a particular emotion to parts of the heart. An example could be gluing on green buttons to represent feelings of anxiety, which may also be green on the heart.

**4.** Explore with the child their "big" and "small" emotions, where these feelings are felt in the body, and what words can be used to name these feelings.

**Note:** If using this intervention in a group or family session, have each member hold up their hearts and describe their art to their group members. The goal is to create a sense of understanding and belonging to their group, as well as validation of the child's emotions.

Created by John, Burr, LCSW

# "THE ME I SEE"

The Me I See is an expressive art therapy technique that guides the child client through creating a self-portrait or visual reflection of their self-interpretation. Creating a visual expression of *Self* can be a telling projection of the characteristics one sees in oneself and often creates an experience of self-exploration. This intervention also can allow an opportunity for the client to share and interpret these discoveries within a clinical setting. Within the process of this exercise, the client will be able to express him/herself creatively and descriptively. The second step of the technique involves instinctually listing defining characteristics of the client's perception of self, personal interests, likes, and more.

This expressive art therapy technique is designed to have multi-layered purpose in a therapeutic setting. It allows the client to express themselves creatively in a therapeutic setting, allowing an alternative method of communicating information between client and clinician. It invites the opportunity for self-reflection and allows the client to explore and reflect on how they view themselves. It also creates an opportunity for sharing to happen between client and clinician which builds trust, advances the therapeutic relationship, and builds rapport.

**SUPPLIES NEEDED:**

Blank paper

Markers, crayons, colored pencils

**DIRECTIONS:**

**1.** Provide your client with a blank piece of paper and creative tools suitable for drawing. These could be markers, pencils, colored pencils, crayons, etc.

**2.** Instruct your client to create a self-portrait. Emphasize that it does not need to be perfect! It can be as abstract or as accurate as the client desires.

**3.** Once the self-portrait is complete, invite the client to share a bit about the drawing and how the child sees him/herself.

**4.** Next, instruct the client to identify defining characteristics, passions, likes, and preferences and list them on the page. Allow the client to be in a quiet space for this process. You may consider designating time in the session to think. It can occur that a client may say, "I don't know any" or "I listed all I can think of." Encourage the client to simply sit and think. Quiet can be positive in a session and allow more time for self-reflection.

**5.** Upon completion of their picture, invite the client to share the finished product.

**6.** Encourage the client to find a place to display the work in a location where he/she will see it regularly.

Created by Melanie Davis, LCMHC

# Chapter 8 — Play Therapy Interventions for Obsessive-Compulsive Disorder

> *When little people are overwhelmed by big emotions, it's our job to share our calm, not join the chaos.*
>
> – L.R. Knost

Obsessive-Compulsive Disorder (OCD) affects one in every 200 children, according to the American Academy of Child and Adolescent Psychiatry (2013). In the most recent edition of the DSM-5®, OCD has been removed from the anxiety disorders chapter and given its own chapter, as understanding of this disorder has broadened. OCD is characterized by the child experiencing obsessions and/or compulsions that result in significant impairment of one's daily functioning. Most children and adolescents recognize that their obsessions and compulsions are not "normal" and may try to hide these behaviors from their parents, as there can be high levels of accompanying shame. Most often, by the time a parent recognizes the level of disturbance the OCD symptoms are causing, these behaviors and thoughts have been occurring for some time. The OCD symptoms not only affect the individual, but impact the entire family system.

---

**OBSESSIONS** are persistent thoughts, images, ideas, or impulses that are considered inappropriate and intrusive. They cause marked distress and anxiety.

**COMPULSIONS** are repetitive behaviors or mental acts engaged in for the purpose of reducing or preventing distress or anxiety.

---

Most cases of childhood OCD include both obsessions and compulsions (Rezvan et al., 2012). Obsessions are typically unwanted and distressing thoughts that include senseless ideas, doubts, and urges, as well as mental images that the person experiences as invasive, uncontrollable, and guilt-provoking (Abramowitz & Jacoby, 2014). Obsessions typically have generalized themes such as contamination, responsibility for causing harm or failing to prevent harm to others, and taboo subjects such as sex, violence, and blasphemy or religious themes. The need for symmetry and organization is also a common theme in obsessive thinking.

| Symptoms of OCD | • Excessive preoccupation with germs, dirt, illness<br>• Expressions of repeated doubts, such as whether the stove is turned off or the door is locked<br>• Intrusive thoughts about a parent getting hurt or sick<br>• Excessive preoccupation with symmetry, order, and exactness<br>• Disturbing thoughts about religious ideas or teachings, such as sin, repentance, and confessions | • Excessive drive to know or remember facts that seem very trivial<br>• Unreasonable attention to detail, including erasing over and over until "perfect"<br>• Excessive worry about something bad happening like a car accident or intruder breaking into home<br>• Fear of leaving the house<br>• Aggressive thoughts and urges (may be more likely in teens) |
|---|---|---|

Obsessions are typically accompanied with various forms of resistance thinking, meaning that there is a sense or thought that the obsession needs to be "dealt with," neutralized, or avoided (Abramowitz & Jacoby, 2014). Compulsions fall into this category, as they are used to prevent or eliminate the obsessive thought. Compulsions often become a ritualized practice that can be extremely-time consuming and overwhelming to the child and parent. These rituals are intended to relieve the anxiety and tension of the obsession, but may do just the opposite and actually intensify it. In other words, the more the child tries to ease the anxiety by engaging in a compulsive behavior, the more the anxiety is experienced (after a momentary feeling of relief). I often use the metaphor of a mosquito bite to explain this process to children and parents. Most of us are unaware we have a mosquito bite until we see it or realize it is there on our body. It typically doesn't itch until we notice it or happen to unconsciously scratch our arm or leg. Once we start scratching the mosquito bite, it feels better momentarily but then it itches even more. The more we scratch, the more it itches! Scratching the bite both relieves the tension and anxiety, but at the same time it increases the itchiness! This is the same thing that is happening inside the brain of a child with OCD!

| Common Examples of Compulsions | • Washing hands excessively, frequently several times a day | • Repeating sounds, words, numbers, or music to self |
|---|---|---|
| | • Repeated checking and rechecking behaviors, such as to ensure stove is turned off or door is locked | • Unreasonably high number of requests for reassurance |
| | • Rigidly follows self-imposed rules of order like arranging personal items (toys, clothes, shoes, etc.) in room in a particular way and becoming very upset if someone disrupts the arrangement | • Long bedtime rituals |
| | • Excessive counting and recounting | • Peculiar pattern of sitting or walking |
| | • Preoccupation with sequencing or grouping objects, such as all things red need to be together | • Retracing over words |
| | • Repeatedly and excessively asking the same questions, requiring the same answer over and over | • Excessive erasures when writing or doing homework |
| | • Repeating words spoken by self or others | • Repeated touching of objects |

Compulsions that are not overtly behavioral are also common. These may include avoidance, distraction, and neutralization strategies. This is a more passive form of compulsion, but the intended outcome is similar: to decrease or eliminate the obsessive thought. An example of this would be a driver who has an obsession of hitting a pedestrian may grip the steering wheel at specific places. In children, this may manifest by magical thinking, as the child may believe that thinking or behaving in a certain way will stop an obsessive thought or fear from coming true.

According to the most recent diagnostic criteria, childhood symptoms do not differ significantly from adult symptoms of OCD. In the new DSM-5® diagnostic criteria, a diagnosis requires the presence of either an obsession *or* a compulsion, which implies that these are independent of one another (Abramowitz & Jacoby, 2014). However, both researchers and clinicians recognize that obsessions and compulsions are typically thematically linked, meaning that there is connection between the thought or fear behind the obsession and the resulting compulsion or behavior manifested (Abramowitz & Jacoby, 2014). For example, a child who experiences obsessions related to fear of germs or contamination often displays excessive hand-washing and/or cleaning rituals.

## FAMILY IMPACT OF OCD

Obsessions and compulsions are extremely time-consuming and result in considerable interference in everyday life. They also can take over most of the family's unwanted and negative attention, as they may impair normal routines, academic functioning, and social relationships. This can significantly impact the family relationship among siblings and in the parent-child relationship. Parents often feel helpless, frustrated, and scared as they are unable to put a stop to the distressing behaviors and thoughts that are continually plaguing the child. They also may not realize the extent of the distress their child is facing until they begin to notice higher utility bills, such as water or electricity, clogged toilets, missing cleaning supplies, or recognize that bedtime is taking much longer than usual. In some children, physical symptoms present initially such as dry, cracked lips and hands from licking or washing too frequently. Depending on the time of year or environmental factors, these symptoms can easily be overlooked as well.

## FAMILY RISK FACTORS

Many children and adults who suffer from OCD also have a high incidence of experiencing depression and anxiety symptoms. A substantial amount of research links OCD to genetics, as it has a high re-occurrence and likelihood of passing down through generations. Other risk factors for developing or increasing the likelihood of pediatric OCD include marital discord, family disorganization, parent-child enmeshment, and the parent's involvement in the OCD rituals (Rezvan et al., 2012). Poor parent-child communication and emotional alienation also are important risk factors, as is poor parental care, which refers to the level of warmth, affection, and support exhibited to children (Yarbro, Mahaffey, Abromowitz, & Kashdan, 2013). Authoritarian and neglectful parenting have also been shown to be high-risk factors.

While there is no known "cause" of OCD, research has found that birth abnormalities, heritability, temper tantrums, neuropsychological status, parent mental health, and family aggregation can play a role in the development of this disorder (Rezvan et al., 2012). Increasingly, research is also considering the role attachment between parent and child plays in the development of OCD, particularly with females (Rezvan et al,. 2012; Yarbro et al., 2013). It has been found that securely attached children are less likely to experience anxiety disorders and symptoms than children who experience insecure attachments. Studies have documented that it is very common for children with OCD symptoms to have parents who are overly intrusive and interfering in many aspects of their lives (Rezvan et al., 2012). This is not to say that parenting (or the parents!) is the root cause of OCD; however, these are risk factors to assess for when a therapist is diagnosing and treating the child with the OCD symptoms, as OCD symptoms may be indicative of a larger family issue rather than a neuropsychological one.

## FAMILY THERAPY

Multiple studies have shown that a cognitive-behavioral treatment approach initially produces rapid results in decreasing the OCD rituals. This is true; however, with children, research also finds that these results are not necessarily long-lasting. Utilizing a prescriptive approach to therapy, incorporating CBT skills in addition to using attachment-based interventions, provides a long-lasting effect on stabilizing OCD and decreasing its impact on daily functioning. It is important while utilizing a prescriptive approach to incorporate known and effective CBT interventions in a treatment plan. Myrick & Green (2012) outline five important steps in treating OCD in children:

1. Externalization of OCD
2. Creating a symptom map and rating symptoms
3. Coping strategies
4. Exposure-response prevention
5. Rewards and goal-setting

Rezvan and colleagues found in their study that, following the termination of therapy services, rates of relapse could be diminished by increasing the parents' participation in the therapy process and by giving the parents as many emotional "tools" as were given to the child (2012). They write, "a well-regulated attachment relationship with parents, which promotes good communication and feelings of trust and closeness towards parents, can help children become emotionally resilient" (p. 411). By improving the attachment between parent and child, the child is better able to self-regulate and ask for help and support, thus alleviating symptoms of OCD.

## Case Study — Sabrina

Sabrina is a nine-year-old child who was referred to counseling after her parents became concerned with some ritualized behaviors and extreme temper tantrums when she was asked to stop. Sabrina's parents report she had "quirky" behaviors growing up, such as needing her room organized a certain way or wearing very tight socks around her ankles that needed to feel "just right." Over time, these "quirks" began concerning her parents, as her emotional response to them intensified. At the time of intake, the "quirks" had turned into licking her hand and wiping it across surfaces, as well as licking others when she came into a room. As you can imagine, this was causing significant disruption across environments, as it would happen not only in her home and with her immediate family, but at school and social activities.

Sabrina not only exhibited strange behaviors, but had intense obsessions regarding relationships, especially with her mother. She was convinced that she was a disappointment to her mother and that her mother wished she didn't have her as a daughter. No amount of reassurance could help decrease these fears and thoughts, nor could spending time together and receiving affection and love from the mother. Sabrina's mother loved her deeply, was involved in her daily life and activities, and was very committed to her. There was a strong attachment and bond between parent and child, but Sabrina's thoughts were not based in the reality of their relationship. She further reported thinking that God knew all her thoughts and no amount of repenting could help him love her because she was "bad." She would spend 30 to 45 minutes a night praying and asking for forgiveness for her "sins." If she was interrupted or found her mind wandering, she had to start all over again, saying the exact words she had previously said in her earlier prayers.

Due to the positive nature of the parent-child relationship, as well as the strain the OCD symptoms were causing in their relationship, Sabrina engaged in both individual and parent-child therapy sessions. In play therapy, Sabrina could explore her fears and feelings of shame, frustration, and resentment to the OCD that she felt was "robbing" her of her life with school, friends, and daily functioning. Her parents could identify and recognize how their responses to the OCD were actually strengthening the OCD cycles and learned skills to help decrease the OCD behaviors while simultaneously strengthening their relationship with their child. Sabrina's treatment team also included her pediatrician, who prescribed a low dose of selective serotonin reuptake inhibitors (SSRI) medication to help manage the depressive and anxious symptoms she experienced. As Sabrina learned skills in recognizing and discerning her OCD thoughts from her "real" thoughts, she was better able to combat her OCD and regain a sense of positive control and feelings of self-worth. This was evident in her relationships across environments, as her daily functioning and her self-esteem improved.

## PLAY THERAPY AND OCD

Research has found that play therapy can be a useful treatment modality in addressing the challenges of OCD. Play therapy allows the child an opportunity to explore feelings of shame, negative self-concept, and treatment resistance in a developmentally-appropriate manner (Gold-Steinberg & Logan, 1999). Utilizing play therapy, therapists can help to normalize their client's fears, thoughts, and feelings and encourage a healthy expression of emotion. Many children who have been diagnosed with OCD experience significant worry and stress that others will think they are weird or crazy and wouldn't want to be friends with them if they found out about their rituals. Play therapy offers the child an opportunity to explore not just the cognitive distortions of the worry, but also give a safe place to honor how these worries impact the child's thinking and relationships now in the present, as well as offer the child new and healthier ways to self-regulate one's affect. Play therapy can also help the child to understand the rationale for the necessary response-prevention techniques and the resulting anxiety this can produce. Allowing time for preparation before play can enable the child to deal more effectively with the stress of the actual interventions (Gold-Steinberg & Logan, 1999).

This was the case with Sabrina and many other children in my practice. When Sabrina was ready to work on decreasing the hand-licking (as well as licking others), initially she would report, "I feel like my hands are on fire if I don't do it," as well as "my hands will catch fire if I don't do this." In play therapy, she could practice breathing through these initial physical feelings and watching her hands not catch on fire (an OCD thought), allowing the sensations to pass as she gained mastery over the impulse to lick her hands and wipe them. This led to an insight for Sabrina as she realized the fear behind the impulse was to wipe away the germs on her hands. First, she had to lick off or "clean" the germs that were "left over" from the previous room when she entered a room. Then she had to wipe off the saliva, which was also covered in germs. If she didn't do this, she could get sick, which could make her mother sick and have to go to the hospital where she could die. Her OCD had tricked Sabrina into believing the only way to keep her mother safe was to lick her hands and wipe them on others! In play therapy, Sabrina could act out these fears, as well as practice ways she could develop mastery over them.

Many play therapy interventions in the following pages are developed to use with parent and child. You can modify them to be appropriate to your work setting, but I would highly encourage you to involve the parent in the play therapy process from the beginning. The underlying attachment issues are core treatment concerns, as is eliminating or decreasing the OCD rituals.

# UNZIPPING ME FROM OCD

This is a guided imagery exercise to help the child begin to discern the OCD thoughts from their "real" thoughts. Many children struggle with understanding if their OCD thoughts are real or reality-based, especially young children whose cognitive development is still rooted in magical thinking. The goal of this intervention is to create a separate, physical, visual "being" that is symbolic of the child's OCD symptoms. In this, the client is de-integrating from his/her OCD symptoms, helping the child to differentiate OCD thoughts from normal, healthy thoughts through externalization processing. The child names the OCD and then uses this in the future as a way to "talk back to," or challenge it. Once the child can recognize the OCD and talk back to it, the child can integrate all the different parts of self and this disorder to create a whole self.

## SUPPLIES NEEDED:

Blank paper
Markers

## DIRECTIONS:

**1.** Instruct the child to get as comfortable as possible. He/she can close their eyes or keep them open, whichever feels best to the child.

**2.** Instruct the child to begin breathing deeply – long, slow breaths – inhaling through the nose and exhaling through the mouth. Take five deep breaths and begin the guided imagery. The child can answer verbally throughout the guided imagery or choose to remain silent. The therapist should pause for 5-10 seconds between each question, giving the child time to visualize or create their OCD character.

**3.** Guided Imagery Exercise:

"I want you to think of your OCD and listen for its voice. What does it sound like? Is it a male or female voice? Does it whisper or yell or talk normally? What color is the voice? If the voice could be some type of shape or object, what does it look like? What is its name?"

**4.** Ask the child to draw a picture of the OCD, using the colors and shapes seen in the guided imagery. Write the name of the OCD on the paper.

# QUIT BUGGING ME!

This intervention is useful for both individual and family therapy. In Quit Bugging Me, the child learns about how different obsessions and their correlating compulsions are meant to relieve the stress and anxiety that the obsessive thought creates. By learning about obsessions and compulsions, the child can begin to identify which obsessions and compulsions he/she engages in and then start to learn different coping strategies to address OCD symptoms. Including the parent in the therapy session also increases their attachment and security, as well as allowing psychoeducation for both parent and child as to the nature of OCD.

**Supplies Needed:**

Blink, Blink, Clop, Clop: An OCD Storybook by E. Katia Moritz, PhD
"Bug Sheet"
Plain paper
Markers

## DIRECTIONS:

**1.** Read Blink, Blink, Clop, Clop: An OCD Storybook with the child and parent. Ideally, the parent will read this book to the child in session together.

**2.** Identify the OCD behaviors and thoughts the animals in the story experience and how they are similar to what the child is currently experiencing with OCD thoughts and behaviors.

**3.** On the bug sheet, write down how OCD "bugs" the child and how he/she can "squish" it.

**4.** Write down different ways the parent can help to squish the OCD (for example, not answering OCD's questions or allowing OCD to trick the child).

_____

_____

_____

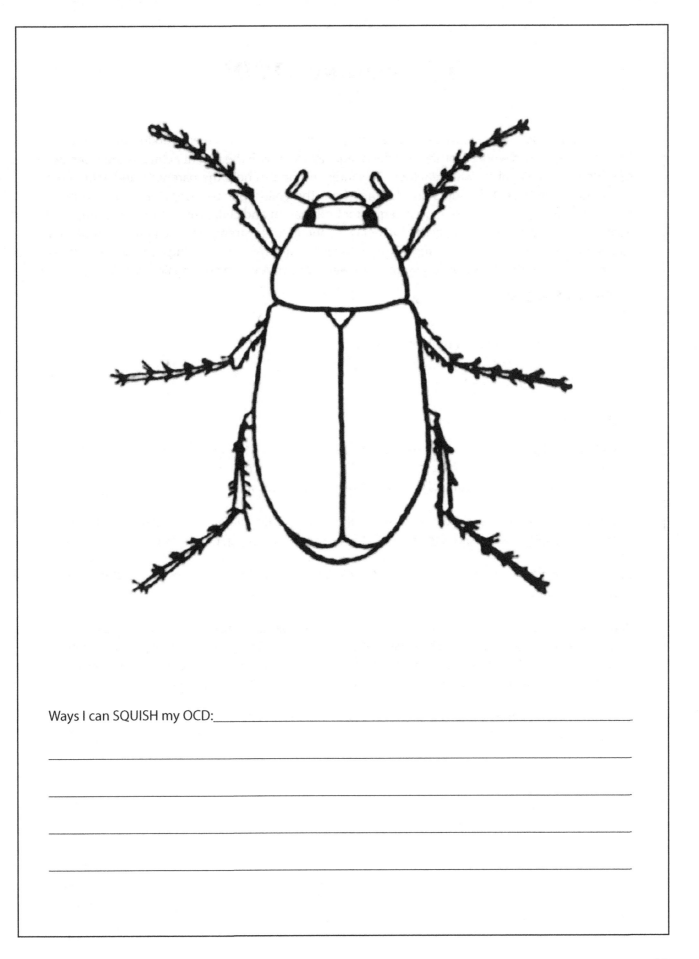

Ways I can SQUISH my OCD:_____

_____

_____

_____

_____

# It's Raining OCD!

This is a fun, delightful parent-child play therapy intervention to use when working through OCD. The parent and child work together to "defend" against OCD, with the parent acting as the protector of the child (instead of the OCD enabler). This intervention can help the parent to understand the magnitude of the OCD thoughts and feelings from the child's perspective, which then helps to increase empathy as well as coping strategies for both parent and child. This activity gives the child a safe space to practice talking back to his/her OCD, and helps to strengthen the family relationship, as parent and child can fight *together* (instead of feeling like they are fighting against each other). This can also help the parent to feel more empowered to assist in the fight against the OCD.

**SUPPLIES NEEDED:**

    Pom-poms
    Plain colored umbrella or umbrella printable
    Permanent marker
    Disney's *A Bug's Life* movie

**DIRECTIONS:**

1. Watch the clip from Disney's *A Bug's Life* where Hopper buries the grasshoppers in grain. Discuss how each pom-pom (e.g., grain seed) is an OCD thought or action. Explore how the OCD can feel overwhelming and frustrating (like getting buried in the seeds).

2. On the umbrella, instruct the parent and child to write different ways they can defend or fight against the OCD such as "I can tell my OCD to stop!" or "I am stronger than my OCD."

3. Demonstrate how easy it is to get "buried" by "raining" down the pom-poms on the child. Gather the pom-poms into a pile.

4. Instruct the parent to hold the umbrella, or if using the paper umbrella, the parent and child can tape the umbrella to a pillow, which will also act as a protection against the pom poms. The parent can also "defend" the child by stating the ways he/she can help the child (what was written down on the umbrella). The therapist will again "rain" the pom-poms over the child.

5. The child is given the umbrella to take home as a reminder of all the ways to defend and fight back together against the OCD.

# Battling OCD Together

In this family-based play therapy intervention, the parent acts as the protector against OCD (instead of the enabler). Parents are often unaware of how their response to the OCD thought or behavior may be perpetuating the OCD cycle. Throughout the therapy process, as parents learn to identify their role in the OCD maintenance, they are empowered to help address and "catch" the OCD *before* the child begins to engage in ritualized patterns. This will help to strengthen the parent-child attachment and help to manage and minimize the child's interfering OCD behaviors.

## SUPPLIES NEEDED:

> Foam sword and shield
> Foam stickers, variety of shapes, sizes, colors
> Permanent marker
> Soft ball

## DIRECTIONS:

**1.** On the sword, instruct the child to write down self-affirming thoughts, such as "I'm stronger than OCD" and "I can talk back to my OCD." If they are younger children, the adult can write down the words for the child, but it is important for the child to come up with these self-affirmations.

**2.** Instruct the parent and child to decorate the shield together. On the shield, instruct the parent and child to write down all of the ways the parent will help the child with combatting the OCD.

**3.** Toss the ball (representing OCD) towards parent and child. As a team, the parent and child work together to block the ball and "fight" the OCD together.

# Chapter 9 — Play Therapy Interventions for Self-Esteem

> *We are never more fully alive, more completely ourselves, or more deeply engrossed in anything than when we are playing.*
>
> – Charles Schaefer

Self-esteem is defined in several different ways, from believing in yourself and your capabilities to believing that you possess self-worth. Developing a healthy self-esteem has long been known to be a crucial aspect of child development. In a healthy trajectory of child development, self-esteem begins in infancy, as the infant is shown love, care, and nurture. In toddlerhood, self-esteem is further enhanced as the parent verbalizes statements such as "Wow! Look at what you can do!" or "Such a big boy! You did that all by yourself!" Children learn early on that they have worth, they matter, and their needs will be met by their loved ones. They learn that they are capable and competent in learning new skills and ways of engaging with their world. They can more easily develop a strong sense of *Self* – the knowledge and security that *I exist and I matter.*

As the child continues to grow and develop, he/she is better able to develop mastery over challenging tasks, withstand peer pressure, and move through disappointment or distress more easily. Possessing high self-esteem is important throughout the lifespan, but most especially during childhood and adolescence. It is in these phases of development where the roots of *Self* are planted and resilience is strengthened. A child with a healthy sense of self is better able to navigate the challenges of elementary and middle school, setting them up to be successful in high school and beyond. In fact, research has shown that a high self-esteem promotes goal making and achieving behaviors, development of appropriately-high levels of expectations of self and others, healthy coping mechanisms, and behaviors that facilitate productive achievement and work experiences (Trzesniewski et al., 2006). Possessing a high self-esteem may also impede mental and physical health problems, substance abuse, and antisocial behaviors (Trzesniewski et al., 2006).

## LOW SELF-ESTEEM

Low self-esteem usually begins to develop in the home environment. Poor or insecure attachment hinders the development of positive self-esteem and self-worth in many ways. A child or teen with low self-esteem feels unworthy, incapable, and incompetent. These negative feelings or lack of self-worth may be compounded by neglectful or abusive parenting practices. Instead of celebrating a child's developmental milestones, if the parent neglects to praise or encourage, or in more severe instances, is abusive or punishing to the child, the ability to form a healthy sense of self or self-esteem is greatly impeded. The child internalizes that he/she is not special or important to the caregivers.

Low self-esteem can be emotionally debilitating in that it keeps individuals from realizing their full potential. This can become negative and self-defeating, as the children caught in this cycle believe that they are unworthy or incompetent, set themselves up for failure, and then become a self-fulfilling prophecy. Children and teens who have low self-esteem are much more likely to experience serious emotional disturbances and develop mental illness as they age, including Conduct Disorder and mood disturbance (Powell, Newgent, & Lee, 2006).

| Children with *High* Self-Esteem: | Children with *Low* Self-Esteem: |
| --- | --- |
| Feel good about themselves | Do not feel good about themselves |
| Feel proud of what they can do | Worry they are not as good as others |
| Believe in themselves (even when they don't always succeed) | Believe they will fail |
| See their own good qualities (such as being kind) | Give up easily |
| Feel liked, loved, and respected | Don't feel liked, accepted, or respected |
| Accept themselves, even when they make mistakes | Blame themselves and fault-find |
| Focus on the positive, rather than the negative | Focus on the negative, rather than the positive |

(Adapted from *The Story of Self-Esteem*, Lyness, 2015)

Although parenting can contribute to the development of low self-esteem, it is important to note that self-esteem is not always a result of neglectful or inattentive parenting. Many children who are treated for mental or emotional health concerns suffer from low self-esteem. It is common for children diagnosed with ADHD (see Chapter 3) to experience low self-esteem, poor peer relationships, and strained family dynamics. Children diagnosed with OCD (see Chapter 8) often are impacted by low self-esteem and believe that they are flawed, unworthy, and unwanted. Children with acting out behaviors, such as Oppositional Defiant Disorder and Conduct Disorder (see Chapter 6), also usually struggle with self-esteem issues, which may be at the root of their acting out and antagonistic behaviors. Low self-esteem is predictive of depression, especially with teen girls (see Chapter 7).

Children who experience loving homes yet struggle socially or are victims of bullying may develop low self-esteem, as their peers' response to them can invalidate their parents' affection or praise. They may come to believe that their parents don't really see the "real" kid inside, who feels worthless, lonely, awkward, isolated, and rejected.

## FAMILY RISK FACTORS

Research has documented that parenting styles impact the development of both implicit and explicit self-esteem in several ways. There are four main styles of parenting commonly referenced in family systems: authoritative, authoritarian, permissive, and uninvolved parenting (Boer & Tranent, 2013). Parents who utilize an authoritative style of parenting clearly define rules and expectations, but also give nurture, love, and support to their child. Children who are raised with an authoritative parent have been shown to have high levels of both implicit and explicit feelings of self-esteem and self-worth (DeHart, Pelham, & Tennen, 2006). This means that they have a core belief of their worth and goodness, which lasts throughout childhood and into adulthood.

Children who are raised in a household with an authoritarian parenting style, however, do not usually develop high levels of self-esteem. Authoritarian parenting is a much more punitive style of parenting that typically involves threats, criticism, and enforcement of strict, dictated rules (DeHart et al., 2006). The child has little input in the family system and is not treated with love, emotional support, or nurture by the parents. In several studies, children raised in authoritarian homes are found to be left lacking in self-esteem and feelings of self-worth and confidence (DeHart et al., 2006; Boer & Tranent, 2013).

Permissive parenting is characterized by inconsistent structure and follow-through with rules and expectations. The parent is generally nurturing and affectionate; however, due to the lack of consistency and ability to regulate the child's behavior, low self-esteem is developed because the child fails to learn appropriate forms of self-regulation and social skills, which may lead to peer rejection and isolation (DeHart et al., 2006).

Uninvolved parents do not monitor or supervise their children. This is a form of neglect where the parent does not offer emotional support, nurture, or care towards the child (Boer & Tranent, 2013). In these types of home environments, there is no celebration of the child's existence or accomplishments. Parents may be actively rejecting towards their child or may simply fail to attend to most parenting responsibilities (Boer & Tranent, 2013). The emotional and physical neglect the child experiences can severely impact the development of a child's sense of self-worth and literal sense of *Self*, as the child learns early on that his/her needs will not be met by the caregiver, and that he/she must not matter enough to the parent to be taken care of.

Uninvolved and authoritarian parenting styles have been shown to be detrimental to the development of self-esteem in children. The therapist must assess the parent-child relationship status and parenting practices when working with a child with low self-esteem. Parental involvement and parent education are highly important.

## Case Study — Ellie

Ellie is a 10-year-old girl who was recently referred to play therapy to address low self-esteem, self-harming behaviors, and overall unhappiness. Her parents referred to her as a "porcupine," as she would rarely allow them to show physical affection to her. Her parents report that Ellie had never really fit in with the neighborhood children, and although she was invited to birthday parties, she was rarely invited to play dates. When her mother has invited children to come to their house to play, she reported that Ellie would become very passive and rarely talk to the other child. Ellie had recently begun scratching her arms with paper clips and, in one instance, a grapefruit knife. In that incident, she drew blood and ran to her father screaming, "This is what you made me do! I hate you!" Her father reported feeling completely overwhelmed and blindsided by her rage and outburst, as he had considered them to have a loving relationship.

In therapy, Ellie would often criticize herself or make self-defeating statements such as "I'm no good" or "I bet other kids would be more fun to be with than me." Initially, Ellie engaged in child-centered play therapy, as this has been demonstrated to increase self-confidence and self-esteem in children. Over time, Ellie began to act more assertively and, instead of asking the therapist what to do, began choosing activities and games in sessions. During this time, she was also learning new skills in increasing her emotional vocabulary and being able to talk about her insecurities and worries. Her parents were invited to attend family play therapy sessions to improve their communication and relationship; they were able to learn new ways to validate and show nurture and affection, which helped to strengthen the parent-child relationship.

Ellie began to be more assertive at home and in school. She would participate in class and engage with her classmates. Her mother reported that the teacher sent an email saying how bright and sparkly Ellie's eyes had become. In therapy, Ellie would relay accomplishments and things she was proud of. When she "graduated" from therapy, Ellie reported feeling confident and secure with herself.

## PARENT INVOLVEMENT

Parents play a critical role in building up and repairing a child's self-esteem and confidence. By providing education to parents about how important their role is in the development and maintenance of their child's healthy development (mentally, physically, and emotionally), they will be better equipped to provide support and nurturing. Referring the parents to an attachment-based parenting class, such as Parent-Child Relational Therapy, may be highly beneficial prior to inviting them to family therapy sessions. Research has documented the importance of parents' ability to show nurture to their child, as this is one of the strongest indicators of a child's development of confidence, self-assurance, and self-esteem.

In therapy, encouraging the parent's participation is also highly important. Play therapy allows for vulnerability and expression of emotions and feelings. Eller (2011) states that play therapy allows adults to decrease their defense mechanisms, which may be highly beneficial, especially for parents who have been taught to parent in a very authoritarian manner and are working on developing a more nurturing approach.

## PLAY THERAPY AND SELF-ESTEEM

Research has shown that play therapy is known to be an effective way to increase self-esteem in children (Siahkalroudi & Bahri, 2015; Landreth, 2002). Play therapy can be effective in treating self-esteem issues in the school setting via group therapy, as well as in traditional settings including group, individual, and family therapy. Child-centered play therapy in particular can improve self-confidence and trust within the child, reduce social isolation, and increase confidence (Siahkalroudi & Bahri, 2015). Also, as the parent-child relationship improves, self-esteem is enhanced. Play therapy allows children to explore the world in a non-threatening and non-judgmental manner, giving them permission to stretch their understanding and improve their appreciation for themselves.

# STARS AND DOTS

This family-based play therapy activity focuses on increasing the child's self-esteem and self-worth. It also helps to identify and decrease negative self-talk, the child's internal belief that a parent is disappointed *because of who he/she is*, not just because of the unwanted behaviors that the child may have engaged in. This activity also helps the parent/caretaker reaffirm love and acceptance of the whole child.

 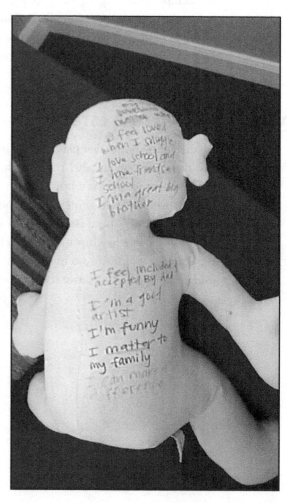

## SUPPLIES NEEDED:

Book *You Are Special* by Max Lucado
Star stickers
Gray dot stickers
Washable markers
My Blanco™ Doll

**DIRECTIONS:**

**1.** Read *You Are Special* by Max Lucado with the parent and child. Ideally, instruct the parent to read to the child if possible. Explore what the dots and stars mean to the child, as well as what it means when the woodcarver says, "You are special because I made you, and I don't make mistakes." Does the child believe it is possible to be special and not a mistake?

**2.** Ask the child to draw each of his/her gray dots (negative thoughts or beliefs about themselves) on My Blanco Doll; gray circle stickers can also be used if desired (if the doll is unavailable, you can use a blank piece of paper or drawing of a gingerbread man for this intervention).

**3.** Instruct the parent/caretaker(s) to draw the child's stars on the doll, representing positive attributes, characteristics, and personality traits they love or honor about the child.

**4.** Explore together the stars and dots that each person has drawn – how they think and feel about each dot and star.

**5.** Turn the doll around. On other side, write down and reframe each dot with an opposite thought that challenges the negative idea. For example, "I don't have any friends at school" can be reframed as "Tommy sits by me at lunch; he likes me" or "I can play with my next-door neighbor, and she is my friend."

# INSIDE/OUTSIDE BOX

This expressive arts-based play therapy intervention is focused on helping identify how an adolescent sees him/herself, as well as how the adolescent thinks others perceive him/her. In this activity, a collage is used as a powerful, symbolic representation of the *Self*. There are many different versions of this activity, and the original author is unknown.

**SUPPLIES NEEDED:**

> Shoebox (multiple sizes)
> Glue
> Scissors
> Various magazines

**DIRECTIONS:**

**1.** The child can choose (or can bring into session) a shoe box with a lid. Instruct the client to cut out different words and pictures from the magazines that represent how he/she believes others view him/her. Glue them into a collage on the outside of the box and lid.

**2.** Explore how others' perceptions may or may not be true and what the client thinks about and feels while looking at the outside "box."

**3.** On the inside of the box, the child repeats the process, using different magazine pictures and/or words. However, the inside of the box should be decorated in a way that represents how the child sees his/her true self and identity.

**4.** Ask the client to share what each picture or word means. Then together, process any thoughts and feelings that may surface.

**5.** Suggested questions:

- How does it feel to look at the outside of your box in comparison to the inside of the box?

- What would you change about or add to the outside of your box, if anything?

- What would you change about or add to the inside of your box, if anything?

**Note:** This may take several sessions to complete. You may want to assign this as "homework" for older children and teen clients.

# DIAMOND IN THE ROUGH

 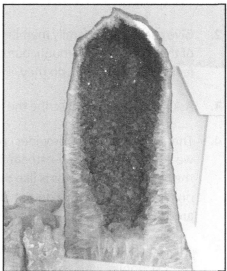

This play therapy intervention uses geodes as a metaphor for the *Self* and is designed to help older children and teens begin to look inwardly at their hidden strengths and positive personal characteristics, finding value in who they are. A geode is a rough, bumpy, asymmetrical, ugly looking rock that holds a surprise internally: Once the geode is cracked open, the inside of the rock is incredibly stunning – filled with crystals, colors, and beauty. Children are able to explore the physical features of the rock and then explore their physical outward features they see in themselves, as well as the internal worth and strengths they possess. This can help to improve a child's feelings of self-worth and self-esteem. "Diamond in the Rough" can be adapted for group, family, or individual therapy.

**Note:** This play therapy intervention is most appropriate for children and teens ages 12+.

## SUPPLIES NEEDED:

> Geode for each person participating in the activity (these can be found in nature or purchased through party supply stores)
> Hammer
> Protective eye wear (for all participants)
> Clean sock

## DIRECTIONS:

1. Discuss with the child how a diamond is created. The therapist may say:

> *When a diamond is first created, it is not shiny and pretty. In fact, a raw diamond is pretty ugly to look at; it actually grows in coal or charcoal. The gem has to be taken out of the coal, cleaned, and polished before it looks like a diamond that you would recognize. People are like this too!*

*We usually look at people, including ourselves, and only look at what we see on the outside and base our beliefs of the value of that person just on their appearance. However, when we look deeper, that is when we see the real value. Sometimes other people can see this before you can, just like the miner who can find the raw diamond in all of the rock and dirt.*

2. Give each child or family member an intact geode. Instruct them to explore the physical features of the rock – feel the rough, bumpy surface. Notice the color and shape of the rock. What does it feel like in their hand, do they like the texture, etc.

3. Ask each person to describe the rock they are holding in both positive and negative terms.

4. The therapist then provides psychoeducation about self-esteem, explaining that when we experience low self-esteem, it can impact the manner in which we view ourselves. Inform the child that each of us is like this geode; on the outside, it is easy to look at our flaws or focus on all of the things we do not like or appreciate about ourselves. We often worry that others are looking at our rough, bumpy surfaces too and may not like what they see.

5. Ask the child to name three good things about him/herself from a physical perspective. If the child struggles with answering this question, it can be helpful for the therapist to say positive statements about the child, such as, "You have a really great smile. It always brightens my day to see it."

6. Instruct the child to put the geode into the clean sock provided. All participants should wear safety goggles. Take the hammer and begin pounding on the rock until it cracks open, then take the halves of the rock out of the sock. Remove your protective eye wear and put the hammer in a safe location.

7. Give the child the geode halves. Explore how the inside of the geode is different from the outside of the geode. Allow the child to physically explore by touching as well as visually exploring the beauty of the inside of the geode. Instruct to child to feel the smooth parts and the crystals and to look at all the different colors that are inside of the rock.

8. Ask the child to describe the inside of the geode. It may be helpful to ask questions such as "What aspects of the geode do you like best?" "Were you surprised to see the inside of the rock is very different from the outward appearance?" You can then explain that our internal worth is like the inside of the geode: Sometimes, because we are only looking at the "ugly or bad" parts of us, we unfortunately forget how beautiful and special we are.

9. Ask the child to name three positive things about him/herself that are internal or personal characteristics (just like the inside of the geode).

10. Give the child the geode to take home as a reminder of his/her inherent worth and value, just like the diamond in the rough.

# GREATNESS STICKS

Greatness Sticks™ are popsicle sticks that are filled with words of positive qualities. The therapist writes words of affirmation, personal strengths, and attributes on the popsicle sticks prior to therapy sessions so they are visual and tangible. This intervention was developed after training in The Nurtured Heart Approach® (Children's Success Foundation, 2015). Greatness Sticks are words that are typed or glued on popsicle sticks but can be written on anything – from shells, to stones, to cut-out hearts – anything you choose. Greatness Sticks help children recognize their strengths and improve their self-confidence and self-esteem. This intervention can be adapted for work with individuals, family, and group therapy.

## SUPPLIES NEEDED:

>   Popsicle sticks
>   Permanent marker
>   Kinetic sand
>   Variety of miniature figurines
>   Blank paper

**DIRECTIONS:**

*CHILD-PARENT THERAPY:*

**1.** Place a cup of Greatness Sticks in front of child and parent/caregiver and ask the parent/caregiver to pick a stick and say how his/her child possesses this quality.

**2.** Instruct the parent and child to stick their Greatness Sticks into the sand.

**3.** If a parent tries to bring up negatives or unhealthy behaviors, it is important to redirect quickly. A parent may ask, "Can we talk about the tantrums and how rude my child is to me?" You should reply, "There are no negative qualities in this activity. It is about the strengths your child has, not the weaknesses."

**4.** Instruct both parent and child to pick a miniature figurine from the sand tray collection that represents them or draw a picture and place it in the sand.

**5.** For those who do not have sand, once the Greatness Sticks are selected, the client draws a picture of how this activity made him/her feel; the Greatness Sticks then surround the picture.

**6.** It is important that you always have blank sticks and invite your clients to add positive qualities to the collection. They can write on the stick with a permanent marker.

**7.** Invite the clients to take their Greatness Sticks home as a transitional object to help them remember their strengths every day.

## INDIVIDUAL THERAPY:

1. Place a cup of Greatness Sticks in front of the child and ask them to pick some (or 'a series of') sticks that represent individual strengths.

2. Instruct the child to stick the Greatness Sticks into the sand.

3. Tell your client to pick a miniature from the sand tray collection that represents them or to draw a picture and place it in the sand.

4. For those who do not have sand, ask the client to draw a picture of how this activity made him/her feel; have the child then place the Greatness Sticks around the picture.

5. It is important for you to always have blank sticks and invite your clients to add positive qualities to the collection. They can write on the stick with a permanent marker.

6. Invite the client to take the Greatness Sticks home as a transitional object to help them remember his/her strengths every day.


## GROUP THERAPY:

This is a powerful activity and a great way to get to know others. Participants are able to see the beauty in others and themselves. This is also a great ice breaker activity and wonderful to use in a staff training to recognize the greatness within the group/company.

1. Split people up into groups of three or four and offer each group a cup of Greatness Sticks; each person will randomly pick two sticks.

2. Each person is then asked, "When you think of this greatness quality, who does it remind you of? Share how this person possesses this quality."

3. The second prompt is to pick another stick and say how he/she personally possesses this quality and why.

Created by Tammi Van Hollander, LCSW,RPT

# In a Nutshell Collage

The In a Nutshell Collage is an expressive art therapy technique that is designed to gather, compile, and reflect a client's current and spontaneous interests. The process is as valuable as the final product. In the first stage of the intervention, clients explore various magazines and media materials (this is a wonderful opportunity for you as the clinician to observe what your client is gravitating towards). Clients are encouraged to take their time in browsing and to not overthink items that catch their eye. Rather, when they see something of interest, they should cut it out and create a collection of spontaneous cutouts.

This approach encourages clients to slow down in pace and make the browsing process one that can become relaxing; it also encourages mindfulness and being present in the moment. The gathering process can span multiple sessions and create an ideal atmosphere for building rapport with clients. The sharing stage of the intervention occurs once the collage is complete and offers a wonderful opportunity for the client and clinician to connect and reflect on the client's interests. In this stage, the clinician has an awesome opportunity to validate, reflect, build rapport, demonstrate active listening, and learn a great deal about a client and his/her personal interests.

**SUPPLIES NEEDED:**

Variety of magazines or other media publications
Scissors
Glue
Blank paper
Picture frame (optional)

**DIRECTIONS:**

1. Conduct the intervention in a space where the client is comfortable and can utilize space as it is needed.

2. Invite the client to browse through a variety of magazines or other media publications.

3. Instruct the client to select images, wording, or other items from media spontaneously, and cut them out.

4. Encourage the client not to overthink items that catch his/her eye, but rather to cut out anything of interest and create a collection of spontaneous cutouts.

5. Allow the client to determine how much time to use to collect clippings and to say when he/she is done.

6. Invite the client to assemble and glue the clippings onto the provided piece of paper.

7. Have inexpensive picture frames available to add value to your client's creation.

8. Once the collage is complete, designate an adequate portion of time to allow the client to share the collage with you. Reflect the client's shared interests as presented through the collage. Encourage clients to display the collage somewhere they will see it in their everyday environments.

Created by Melanie Davis, LCMHC, NCC

# LIKE A GIRL TECHNIQUE

Adolescence can be a challenging time for girls, as this is a time when self-esteem and self-worth can plummet. Today's teens are met with a barrage of negative messages from social media, television, and unfortunately, sometimes from the adults in their world. Too often, teen girls are discouraged from pursuing classes in math and science, or ridiculed by their peers for being "too smart" if they participate in class. Counteracting this negative messaging is an important part of helping to increase self-esteem and build confidence in your teen clients.

In this expressive arts technique, we are incorporating media into the play therapy intervention. This can be useful for individual, family, or group work.

## SUPPLIES NEEDED:

Blank paper

Scissors

Markers

Tape

Craft and/or scrapbooking paper

Yarn

## DIRECTIONS:

**1.** With your client, watch the *Always Like a Girl* YouTube video. This can be found at
https://www.youtube.com/watch?v=XjJQBjWYDTs

**2.** Explore with your client what negative messages they heard in the YouTube video. Questions you may want to process:

- How does it feel to you when someone says something such as, "You throw like a girl"?

- How do you think each of these teens felt about themselves when they were showing you how "a girl" runs, throws, walks, etc.?

- If you were one of these girls, would these messages make you change the way you act or felt about yourself?

**3.** Direct your client to make a set of paper doll chains.

**4.** Give your client a full-size piece of blank paper (8½ x11 works well or the paper can be larger). Cut each sheet of paper in half length-wise.

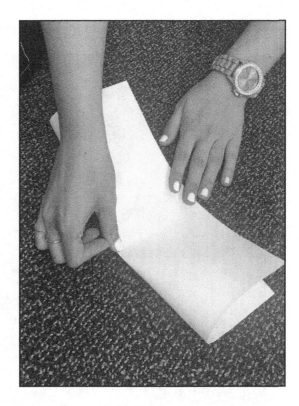

**5.** Fold each piece of paper into equal sections accordion-style:

- Fold the strip in half, matching edges and making a sharp crease.

- Fold one edge back to meet the fold just made, and crease. Turn the paper over and repeat with the other edge. Now you have four equal sections—continue folding to make eight sections.

- Fold the top layer back to meet the center fold, turn over and repeat.

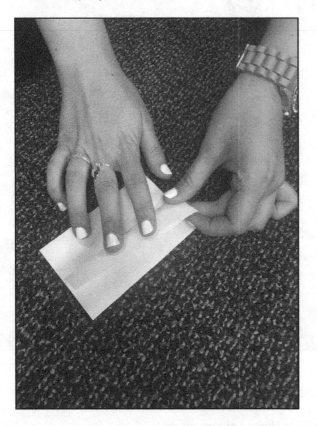

- Open the center fold like a book. There are three layers on each side with a single layer in the center.

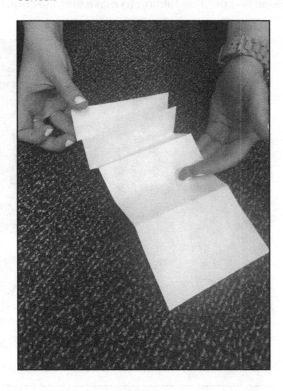

- Fold one side of three layers in to meet the center fold. Repeat with the other side.

- Fold the center fold back to complete the accordion folds.

6. With the cut edge of the folded strip to the right, draw half of a doll along the left (folded) edge with arms extending to the cut edge.

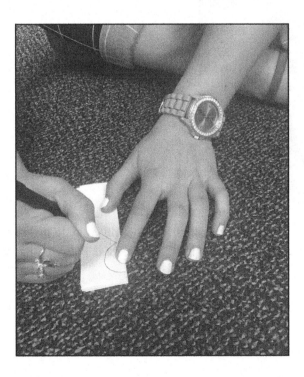

**7.** Hold the folded strip firmly and cut carefully around the doll outline. **Do not cut along the folds.**

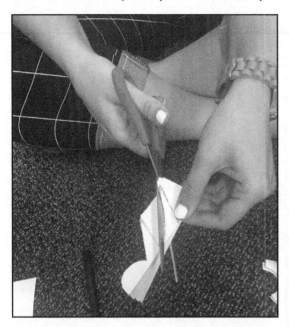

**8.** Unfold the paper strip to reveal your chain of dolls.

**9.** Instruct your client to open the paper doll chain. On each doll, the client will create a doll that is symbolic of the different negative messages she has heard or felt about herself. Provide plenty of expressive arts and craft materials to your client.

**10.** Explore the different meaning of each doll and how this has made her feel about herself and her abilities.

**11.** Repeat the instructions in steps 5-8 to make another set of dolls. On this set, each doll will represent a positive message or empowerment. Once the set of dolls is created, instruct your client to create a message of empowerment or positive things she believes about herself.

**12.** Explore the following questions with your client:

- What feelings do you feel when you look at these dolls with the positive messages?
- What can you do that you are most proud of? If you can't think of anything, what do you want to be proud of in the future?
- Which of these dolls speak to you the very most?

**13.** Ask your client to tape the hands of the negative and positive dolls together, to represent that each of us has good/bad parts of self and that these positive and negative messages matter. The positive messages can either overlay the negative messages, representing the strength of the positive or they can join hands in a circle to represent and honor the good and bad thoughts and feelings of the client.

# SHAME SHIELDS

Shame is a universal affect that impacts all humans across ages and stages. It is particularly powerful and present when treating issues of trauma and abuse. Helping young (and older) clients understand the definition of shame, how it affects their behaviors and relationships, and how it impacts their self-esteem and feelings of self-worth is a crucial aspect of treatment - particularly when working with sexual abuse and trauma.

As humans, we naturally shy away from and try to avoid this intense emotion and create defense mechanisms to protect ourselves. In this intervention, the client not only identifies where/how/why they are experiencing feelings of shame, but also learns how to fight back against these messages of negative self-talk. This creates a feeling of empowerment and permission to be human. The client learns to tolerate uncomfortable emotions while learning new coping strategies to protect and defend their hearts in a healthy, proactive manner. The psychoeducation material on shame comes from the book *Daring Greatly* by Dr. Brené Brown. This intervention can be used in individual, family, or group play therapy.

## SUPPLIES NEEDED:

Poster board

Aluminum Foil

Markers

Magazines

Expressive arts materials such as googly eyes, pipe cleaners, fabric scraps, etc.

Glue

Scissors

## DIRECTIONS:

**1.** Provide one sheet of poster board to your client and instruct them to draw a shield on the poster board. This shield can be any shape or size. As the client is drawing the shield, you may want to discuss with them the definition of shame and how it manifests internally. You could say something such as, "*Shame is a feeling that all humans experience from time to time. This is often a feeling resulting from an experience where we feel "bad" or believe that we did something "bad," which tricks our brain into believing that we are unworthy, unlovable, and unwanted.*" You may want to ask the following questions as the client creates their shield:

- When is a time you have felt shame?
- Where do you feel this feeling in your body?
- What do you do when this feeling happens?

**2.** The client then cuts out their shield and covers it in aluminum foil.

**3.** Instruct the client to create a collage representing their feelings or experiences of shame on one half or section of the shield. As they are creating their collage, you may want to say the following, *"Over time, shame can grow into a giant feeling inside of us. It becomes our shame monster. Each of us tries to protect ourselves from feeling shame. There are three main ways we fight our shame: the first way is we may hide or try to keep secrets from others, because we are afraid if our loved ones knew about our secret, they wouldn't love us anymore. The second way we try to fight our shame is to move towards others by trying to please everybody and keep everybody happy - even if that means not taking care of ourselves and our own personal happiness. The third way people try to fight shame is by using shame! We try to make other people feel just as bad as we are feeling."*

You may want to process with your client which of these strategies they have used in the past or currently use to protect themselves when they experience feelings of shame.

**4.** Process with your client healthy ways to manage feelings of shame. You may say something like: *"We know that shame grows with secrecy and can feel bigger than you! Shame hates words wrapped around it and can only shrink when it is surrounded with empathy. Shame tricks us into believing that if other people knew, they wouldn't love us anymore. The opposite of this is true! When our shame is treated with empathy, it's impossible for it to continue to grow bigger and instead it shrinks down in size. The more we can talk about our feelings of shame and use our words to talk about and explore it, the smaller the feeling becomes, especially if those around us can be supportive listeners."*

**5.** Ask your client to create a picture or representation of how they can fight their shame in a healthy or empowered manner using collage or other expressive arts on the opposite side of their shield. They may want to make a list of people who they can trust to be supportive and empathic listeners and glue that somewhere on their shield.

**6.** The client can take their shield home with them to remind them of how they can fight their shame monster in a healthy manner and to remind them about the power of empathy in fighting shame.

# Chapter 10 — Play Therapy Interventions for Improving Social Skills

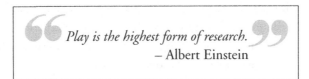

> " *Play is the highest form of research.* "
> – Albert Einstein

Many school-age children struggle with understanding and engaging in positive, healthy, and age-appropriate social skills. A child's individualized process of neurological, biological, and emotional development is impacted by both environmental and genetic issues. A child who is born with developmental, cognitive, and physical disorders may struggle with learning appropriate social skills. A child who has been impacted by abuse and trauma (see Chapter 11) may experience significant problems with brain development, which detrimentally impacts the ability to read and understand others' social cues, as well as act in an age-appropriate manner.

Children who have been diagnosed with a Disruptive Behavioral Disorder, such as Oppositional Defiant Disorder (see Chapter 6), typically struggle significantly in social situations, as they experience ongoing peer rejection due to acting out and aggressive behaviors. The ability to self-regulate and control impulses is also an issue of neurological development. Children who are diagnosed with Autism Spectrum Disorder (see Chapter 5) experience social challenges including not being able to understand the feelings, thoughts, and intentions of self and others (Beaumont & Sofronoff, 2008). In addition, many outside environmental factors impact a child's ability to regulate their emotions, act in an age-appropriate manner, and cope with daily stressors. Peer issues, such as bullying, rejection, isolation, and the resulting self-esteem issues also impact a child's ability to pick up on and respond to social cues appropriately.

The behavioral issues that typically coincide with poor social skills are often cause for concern not just for parents, but for educators as well. Many teachers and school administrators struggle with finding the right balance between meeting the needs of the individual student versus meeting the needs of the classroom environment. They also might not know how to best set a boundary to manage acting-out behavioral issues appropriately. School counselors have often shared that their primary referral problems consist of behavioral issues and poor self-regulation of certain students. Parents report struggling with balancing the desire to "rescue" their child from awkward situations with letting him/her try to navigate social experiences alone. They can also have feelings of anger and helplessness as they watch their child miss out on social opportunities because of poor social skills or behaviors.

Clinicians can utilize both a non-directive and a directive approach in implementing a social skills group therapy, as both have been shown to be highly effective in producing a positive change in both behavioral and emotional regulation, as well as an increase in emotional intelligence and empathy skills (Garza & Bratton, 2005; O'Connor & Stagnitti, 2011). It is developmentally appropriate when engaging with preschool through kindergarten-age children to use a child-centered or non-directive group modality. Many of the interventions in this chapter will be directive play therapy interventions, as they can be easily duplicated and implemented in a variety of situations from school-based counseling to outpatient services.

## PARENT INVOLVEMENT

Parents play a critical role in helping their child successfully implement the new social skills he/she is learning across environments. It is also highly important for the clinician to engage with the parents of the group participants, informing them of the social skills being taught during the week and how the parent can help fortify the child's knowledge and practice of the social skill. One method that can be effective in including and enhancing the therapeutic alliance with parents is to send home a weekly parent newsletter documenting what was learned in the social skills group, with ideas for practicing the social skills throughout the week (see example handout on pg. 123); and then offering to meet with the parent outside of group to discuss concerns and observations.

At times, the parent may also lack critical social skills and may not have a full understanding of why the child needs to attend the social skills group or how it can help in the home. Providing psychoeducation to the parents about how this group can help *them* to learn to manage difficult behavioral issues can benefit the child (and the whole family system) in the long run. Meeting with the parents prior to beginning group therapy is important, as it gives the clinician a chance to assess the family's environment and level of functioning.

## Case Study — Alex

Alex is a nine-year-old boy who was recently referred to the social skills group at a local outpatient community mental health center. Alex's parents report that he was born with no complications, meeting all his developmental milestones on time. Alex is an only child and has been raised socializing with his parents' adult friends. He can hold long conversations about science, social policy, and math with adults, but when he is around same-age peers, Alex will shut down and not engage with the other children.

He is very bright at school and does well academically; his grades show that he is well above average. However, he will often ask his teacher if he can spend recess with her instead of going out to play. When he is forced to go outside, his teacher notices he will keep to himself and occupy himself by looking at bugs or the trees or playing with pebbles by the door. He rarely engages with others, even if kids approach him first.

# SOCIAL SKILLS GROUP

Date: _____

Welcome Parents!

We are so excited to have your child in our social skills group! We will be learning many new, fun ways to engage with others! Some of the skills we will be learning are:

- Making and keeping friends

- Delayed gratification

- Empathy development

- Personal space bubbles

This week we will be working on _____. Some fun ways you can help your child this week with this new skill are:

**1.** Practice walking up to others and introducing yourself, giving eye contact, and shaking their hand.

**2.** Make faces in the mirror together. Try to make sad faces, funny faces, mad faces, etc., and see if you and your child can guess the emotion the other person is showing.

**3.** Continue practicing personal space bubbles. Get a hula-hoop and practice standing next to the bubbles but not inside each other's bubbles. You may want to shake and groove in your hula hoops together, too!

We are so excited for our next group meeting! Next week, we will be learning about the social skill of _____.

We look forward to seeing you soon! If you have any questions or concerns, please remember these are important to me! Please make an appointment with our office manager _____ and we can schedule a time to talk through these issues.

Warmly,

# Case Study — Jeffery

Jeffery is a 10-year-old boy who was recently discharged from the hospital following a life-threatening illness that resulted in the loss of sight for several weeks. During his hospitalization, he was conscious and could hear everything around him, but could not see. Following his discharge, he was unable to go to school due to the high risk of disease from his impaired immune system. He spent several weeks home alone recuperating. He reports feeling lonely and isolated and that he doesn't fit in with his friends anymore. Jeffrey thinks that his illness has taken all his friends away, and he feels angry, sad, and lonely. He has recently begun acting in a verbally, and at times physically, aggressive manner towards his parents and younger sister.

# Case Study — Alice

Alice is a seven-year-old girl who has been diagnosed with Autism Spectrum Disorder. Although she is relatively high functioning, she struggles significantly in understanding social cues and does not understand why she does not have any friends even though she desires to have them. Alice is charming and delightful when she is first introduced to the group facilitator. However, as the other participants join the group, Alice's affect changes, and she starts speaking in a childish high-pitched voice. She will poke others on the arms and faces. She will scoot closer to a child who just tried to create physical distance from her, and she blurts out thoughts that are out of context with the conversation happening around her. At the end of the group, Alice began meowing and crawling around on her hands and knees and tried to lick the participants as they were leaving.

## PLAY THERAPY AND SOCIAL SKILLS

Play-based social skills groups have been shown to be highly beneficial for children who experience social anxiety, ADHD, autism, Down syndrome, and a host of other issues such as emotional and behavioral disorders that may impact a child's ability to navigate the world effectively (Barry & Burlew, 2004; Quirmbach, Lincoln, Feinberg, Ingersoll, & Andrews, 2008; O'Connor & Stagnitti, 2011; Gresham, Cook, & Crews, 2004). Research demonstrates that social skills training is effective for both externalizing and internalizing behaviors, such as aggressiveness and antisocial behaviors, in addition to social withdrawal and isolation (Gresham et al., 2004). By providing an opportunity for a child to engage in a prosocial manner with his or her peers, the social skills group experience can facilitate an enhanced understanding of how to engage with others, whether it is learning social skills in how to introduce him/herself to a new person or learning how to regulate emotional responses when feeling overwhelmed, frustrated, or unsure. Many of the interventions in Chapter 5 are useful for all social skills groups and can be adapted to work with a variety of social skills groups.

# M&M FEELINGS GAME

The purpose of this play therapy technique is to facilitate a conversation about "How am I feeling today?" in either an individual, family, or group therapy session. This activity is a great ice-breaker, as well as a way to build rapport between group members. There are many different varieties of this game, and the original creator is unknown.

## SUPPLIES NEEDED:

Multi-colored candy pieces, such as M&M's® chocolate candies

## DIRECTIONS:

**1.** Instruct the group members to sit in a circle facing one another. Give each member a handful of colorful candies. Instruct them not to eat the candy at this time.

**2.** Instruct each member to choose a feeling to correlate with each color of the candy in their hand. It is up to them to make a personal meaning for each color (for example, a red M&M is equated with feeling mad).

**3.** Each group member describes one time they have felt this color/feeling within the past few days. The other group members are instructed to not interrupt or debate this feeling or experience. If they have felt similarly, they can raise their hands or give a thumbs-up.

**4.** Continue taking turns in the circle until all group members have been able to express their feelings using the M&M's® in their hand with the different colors/emotions selected.

**5.** If they choose to, the group members can then eat their candy.

# Dr. Gary's Therapeutic Cootie Game

Over 50 million copies of The Cootie Game have been sold since it was introduced in 1949. It is a great preschool game where the child creates a Cootie bug. The game consists of a picture board that depicts all the game parts, Cootie body parts (body, head, antenna, proboscis, eyes, six legs), and a die.

This modified version of The Cootie Game introduces a therapeutic element of learning healthier social skills to use in everyday life. The version described below focuses on social skills and depression, but any story can be written to work on any number of issues and challenges.

The object of the game is for each of the players to construct their own Cootie. The first player to do so wins the game. In the therapeutic version, it is not necessary to have a winner. The goal is to complete the story.

## SUPPLIES NEEDED:

The Cootie Game

**GAME PLAY:** Each part of the body is identified by a number as follows: 1–Body, 2–Head, 3–Antenna, 4–Eye, 5–Proboscis, and 6–Legs. There are two ways to begin the game. Each player rolls the die once and the high score starts the game, or the youngest child may go first.

Each player tries to get the body of the Cootie by rolling a "one" spot. If successful, he/she gets a free roll of the die to try for the head. The body and the head must be obtained in the order named, before any other parts of the Cootie can be attached. The legs, eyes, antenna, and proboscis can be acquired in any order; all are eligible after the body and head are obtained. The player loses the die when they fail to roll the number for an eligible part that they have not yet acquired. For example, if the player rolls a four and already has the eyes, then the die gets passed to the next player. If the player rolls a four and doesn't yet have the eyes, the player will pick them up and roll again.

One body, one head, eyes, two antennae, one proboscis, and six legs are required to make a complete Cootie.

In the therapeutic version, parts are acquired, but must be added to the Cootie in order, so that a story can be told that makes sense. If a part is acquired out of order (for example, a leg before Cootie has a proboscis), the part is picked up and set aside until it can be added.

## DIRECTIONS:

**1.** Direct the children to sit in a circle. Each child will have a turn to roll the die, and the child with the highest number rolled will begin the game. Rotating clockwise around the group, every child will take a turn.

**2.** Follow the prompts for the social skills story to create the Cootie.

**3.** After the Cootie bugs have been completed, ask the children the following prompts:

- What did you like best about this game today?

- What was the hardest part about playing this game today?

- What social skill did we learn about today?

- How can you use this social skill during the week?

## SOCIAL SKILLS STORY

When a "1" is rolled and the body is acquired, each player says: "Cootie wants to play."

When a "2" is rolled and the head is acquired, each player says: "Cootie wants to play with

_____" (choose a fellow player, a peer, or a sibling).

Players are now eligible to acquire body parts in any order, but they are added to Cootie in the order listed below.

When the eyes are acquired, each player says: "Cootie is going to look at _____ when Cootie speaks. Cootie is going to look at _____ when _____ talks," and the player attaches the eyes to Cootie. If the player has already acquired the antenna, then that can now be added.

When the antenna is acquired and added, each player says: "Cootie is going to listen carefully when _____ talks" as they attach the antenna to the head.

When the proboscis is acquired, each player says: "Cootie is going to keep his/her tongue, feet, and hands to itself when she plays" as the proboscis is added to the Cootie.

- Each leg represents a skill or affirmation, depending on the child's needs. Here are some examples:
- Leg 1: Cootie says, "Do you want to play with me?"
- Leg 2: Cootie tells itself, "I won't get mad if someone says no; I'll find someone else to play with."
- Leg 3: Cootie says, "You're the guest. What do you want to play?"
- Leg 4: Cootie tells itself, "Make sure your friend is having fun."
- Leg 5: Cootie says, "Thanks for playing with me. I had fun!"
- Leg 6: Cooties tells itself, "I did a good job taking turns and sharing today."

After each Cootie is completed, the story is retold, repeating each statement as the appropriate body part is pointed to.

*Here's an alternative version for a depressed child:*

When a "1" is rolled and the body is acquired, each player says, "Cootie doesn't want to be sad and bored today."

When a "2" is rolled and the head is acquired, each player says, "Cootie is going to think of three things it can do today" (the therapist can prompt the child or make suggestions).

When the eyes are acquired, each player says, "Cootie looks for Mom (Dad, teacher, sibling) and gives them a hug," and the player attaches the eyes to Cootie. If the player has already acquired the antenna, then that can now be added.

When the antenna is acquired and added, each player says, "Cootie tells itself one thing it likes about its life" as they attach the antenna to the head. (The therapist can ask the child to identify that one thing, or make a suggestion).

When the proboscis is acquired, each player says, "Cootie enjoys tasty food. The tastiest food I had this week is _____" as the proboscis is added to the Cootie.

Again, each leg represents a skill or affirmation, depending on the child's needs. Here are some examples:

- Leg 1: Cootie says, "I don't have to be bored. I can find something to do."
- Leg 2: Cootie tells itself, "I don't have to be sad all the time. I can be happy when _____."
- Leg 3: Cootie says, "Two things I like about my life are _____ and _____."
- Leg 4: Cootie tells itself, "The person who can help me when I'm sad is _____."
- Leg 5: Cootie says: "I am beautiful. And then Cootie says it again really loud, I AM BEAUTIFUL!"
- Leg 6: Cootie tells itself, "I am good at _____."

Again, after each Cootie is completed, the story is retold, repeating each statement as the appropriate body part is pointed to.

*Here's a story for non-compliance, with a focus on "listening the first time."*

When a "1" is rolled and the body is acquired, each player says, "Cootie listens the first time."

When a "2" is rolled and the head is acquired, each player says, "Cootie is guessing what its Mom and Dad are going to tell him to do today." The therapist asks the child to guess.

When the eyes are acquired, each player says, "Cootie looks at its mom's (or dad's or teacher's) face when she tells Cootie what to do." If the player has already acquired the antenna, that can be added now.

When the antenna is acquired and added, each player says, "Cootie listens very carefully so that Cootie can repeat what it heard" as they attach the antenna to the head.

When the proboscis is acquired each player says, "Cootie tells its mom (dad, teacher) what it is going to listen to today" as they add the proboscis to Cootie. The therapist can encourage the child to guess what that might be.

As noted previously, each leg represents a skill or affirmation, depending on the child's needs. Here are some examples:

- Leg 1: Cootie says, "I don't want to brush my teeth, but I will."
- Leg 2: Cootie tells itself, "I wish I didn't have to go to bed, but I will."
- Leg 3: Cootie says, "I am going to listen the first time again!"
- Leg 4: Cootie tells itself, "Listening the first time is easy today."
- Leg 5: Cootie says, "I had a good day. I listened the first time."
- Leg 6: Cooties tells itself, "I am good at listening the first time."

Again, after each Cootie is completed, the story is retold, repeating each statement as the appropriate body part is pointed to.

Created by Gary Yorke, PhD, RPT

# THE WORK IT OUT GAME

The Work It Out Game gives children an opportunity to develop and practice prosocial skills including empathy and moral development. They will practice making new friends and learn to engage in appropriate conversations. Children will role play different social interactions using the marshmallow people that each child can design. The marshmallow people act like puppets, giving children a fun, playful way to role play with one another. The idea of using marshmallow people as "puppets" comes from Liana Lowenstein's intervention *My Parents Argue and I Feel Stuck in the Middle* (Lowenstein, 2006). This is a very interactive intervention within the group so get ready for lots of giggles, some mess, and yummy treats to follow their hard work!

## SUPPLIES NEEDED:

 Large marshmallows
 Stick pretzels
 Gel frosting or frosting pens
 Tarp (to protect flooring/carpet)

## DIRECTIONS:

**1.** Instruct the children to sit in a circle. Give each child six big marshmallows and 10 pretzels. Instruct the children not to eat the food at this time.

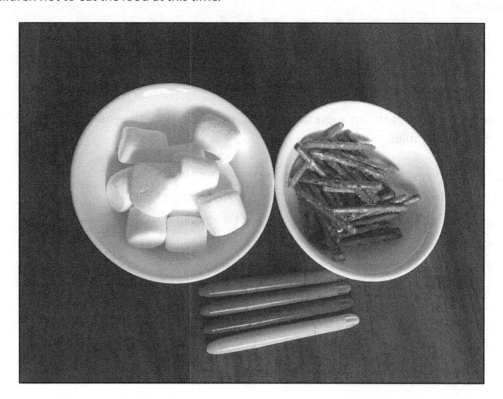

**2.** Instruct the children to take one marshmallow and push one pretzel halfway through the marshmallow. Add a second marshmallow at the other end of the pretzel to make a dumbbell shape.

**3.** Poke one stick into each side of the second marshmallow. You may want to break it in half if you would like shorter arms for the marshmallow person.

**4.** Poke one stick into each side of the lower half of the second marshmallow to make the legs.

5. Create a "face" on the top marshmallow using the gel or frosting pens to decorate. Attach the head to the body by breaking a pretzel stick in half and sticking it into the main body and pushing the "head" on top of it.

6. Set aside and complete instructions again for a second marshmallow person (each child should now have two marshmallow people).

7. Instruct the group to pair up with a buddy (can be a trio if necessary) for the remainder of the session. Each pair is given a set of social skills cards that describe different social scenarios. After they have read the card, each pair will use their marshmallow people to act out how to best address the cue card scenario in a positive, prosocial way.

8. Following the completion of the card game, each child can eat their marshmallow people or take them home if desired.

# SOCIAL CUE CARDS

**1.**
Johnny and Seth are sitting at the table eating their school lunches. They notice Joey sitting all alone at the end of the table. What should they do?

**2.**
Sarah and Jane are playing hopscotch at recess. They have thrown the disc a little too hard and too far, and it accidentally hits one of their classmates. What are three things they can do that could help their classmate feel better?

**3.**
Zachary and Isaiah have been best friends since kindergarten. Recently, Isaiah has begun playing with different friends at recess, and Zachary feels left out. How should Zachary handle this situation with his friend?

**4.**
Eliza is the new kid in school. She is very shy and feels nervous to introduce herself to the class. What social skill could she use to make a new friend?

**5.**
Marissa notices that Jake often looks sad and doesn't join in the fun at recess. She watches him stand by himself and look at the ground. What could Marissa do to help him feel better?

**6.**
Matt and Miguel are constantly teasing Sammy in class. He has asked them to stop several times without success. What are three things Sammy can do in this situation to help himself?

# DR. GARY'S CANDY LAND™
## "THERAPY" GAME

This social skills game is great for group and family therapy. As players move around the board, they get to answer a question from the stack of cards. Participants get to practice social skills of taking turns, listening without interrupting, and distress tolerance as they never know if they are going to be sent backwards or get stuck on sticky licorice to lose a turn!

**SUPPLIES NEEDED:**

> Candy Land™ game
> Collection of prompt cards

**DIRECTIONS:**

**1.** Have each player pick their game pawn. The youngest player gets to go first, moving in a circular pattern throughout the group.

**2.** Players move around the Candy Land board in the standard way, following the game instructions for how many spaces they may move forward or backwards.

**3.** When you land on a square that matches the color of your pawn, you get to pick a card from the deck and answer the question or act out the prompt. For example, if your pawn is red and you land on a red square, you would then answer the question from the game prompts.

**4.** The "winner" of the game arrives to the Candy Land castle first.

Created by Gary Yorke, PhD, RPT

# Cooperation and Compliance

**1.**

Name one rule you really don't like. Can you think of a good reason for that rule?

**2.**

When is it hard to share or take turns? What would make it easier?

**3.**

Give an example of when you listened the first time. Tell yourself "good job!"

**4.**

Pretend you're the boss. Tell the other players a good way to be cooperative with their Mom or Dad.

**5.**

Do your parents ask you to try new things? Tell about a time you tried something new and you liked it.

**6.**

Pretend you're helping somebody. What are you doing for them?

**7.**

Why don't children want
to play with someone
who is bossy?

**8.**

What are the rules
for playing outside
at school?

**9.**

What are the rules
when a friend comes
to your house?

**10.**

What gets your
Mom mad?

**11.**

What gets your
Dad mad?

**12.**

Say one thing you
don't like to be told
to do.

**13.**

Say why children don't like having their toys grabbed.

**14.**

What does cooperation mean?

# ANXIETY

**1.**

Name something you are afraid of. Is that real or pretend?

**2.**

Who can you talk to when you are scared?

**3.**

Who keeps us safe in the community (outside our house)?

**4.**

What is something an adult told you when you were afraid? Will it help to say that to yourself next time you are afraid?

**5.**

Some people think you should practice being brave to get over your fears. What is something brave you did even though you were afraid?

**6.**

Think of a time you were really happy. Talk about it. Pretend you are afraid and talk about the time you were really happy. Do you think that will help next time you're afraid?

**7.**

Draw a picture of something you're afraid of. Now say why you shouldn't be afraid of that thing.

**8.**

Sing the happiest or silliest song you know. Do you think you can sing that song when you're scared?

**9.**

Say something you are afraid of. How could you practice being brave when you are afraid of that thing?

**10.**

Pretend you are afraid. Take a big breath. Blow the fear out S-L-O-W-L-Y.

**11.**

What is the safest place in your house? If you close your eyes, can you imagine that place?

**12.**

A boy did not like it when his mother went out or left him at school. She gave him something special, which belonged to her. He was able to hold on to it until she came back. Guess what it was.

**13.**

Being scared may be a clue that you are in danger. Remember the last time you were scared. Were you in danger?

# DEPRESSION

**1.**

Name something that makes you feel happy. Is that something you can do when you are sad?

**2.**

Who helps you when you feel sad? What do they say?

**3.**

Sing a silly or happy song. When you sing that song, do you feel sad, glad, mad, or scared?

**4.**

Name something that you really like about your life.

**5.**

Did you ever try something, over and over, and finally do it (like write your name or remember how to count)?

**6.**

Is it okay to make mistakes?

**7.**

Say "I feel good!" three times. What do you like about yourself?

**8.**

A boy thought going to school was no fun. Tell him what you do at school that is fun.

**9.**

A girl did not like to play alone. Tell her what you like to do when you play alone.

**10.**

A boy was sad, so he asked his family members to give him hugs. Who can you ask for hugs?

**11.**

What could you make for a parent? How would you feel when you gave it to a parent? Sad, glad, mad, or afraid?

**12.**

What is the best thing that ever happened to you?

**13.**

Pretend you just got sent to timeout. Say "I can handle this. I'm a good person and I'll stay out of trouble next time."

# SOCIAL SKILLS

**1.**

Cooperate means to share, take turns, and to do what the other person wants. When do you cooperate?

**2.**

When is it hard to cooperate? What would make it easier?

**3.**

What are some words you can use when you want to play with someone?

**4.**

What is a good way to decide who goes first?

**5.**

When is it a good idea to take turns?

**6.**

Pretend you're helping somebody. What are you doing for them?

**7.**

Ask another player to tell you about their favorite meal. Listen carefully, and then tell them what they said.

**8.**

Pretend you're talking to a new student. What are some polite and friendly things you can say?

**9.**

Ask another player to tell you about a worry or a problem. Tell them what they said and one thing they can do about their problem.

**10.**

What are the rules for playing outside at school?

**11.**

What are the rules when a friend comes to your house?

**12.**

Ask another person to stare at your nose. Does it look like they are making eye contact?

**13.**

Some people divide things when they want to share. What are some things that can be divided?

**14.**

Some people trade when they want to share things. What are some things that can be traded?

**15.**

In a nice way, ask another player to play Candy Land with you.

**16.**

What is something that is hard to do? Ask another player for help when you do that thing.

**17.**

Grab another player's piece. Now give it back and say, "I'm sorry, I won't do that again."

# LOW FRUSTRATION TOLERANCE

**1.**

What makes you really mad? When you feel that mad, where can you go so you don't get into trouble?

**2.**

When something gets too hard, some people get mad. Pretend you're telling a mad person to "take a break, and calm down." How long should their break be?

**3.**

Pretend you're mad. Now do a mad dance and shake it all out!

**4.**

Some people like to laugh at other people. Say, "Please stop laughing at me – that hurts my feelings."

**5.**

Pretend someone is laughing at you and they won't stop. Name an adult who can help you.

**6.**

Pretend you're going to hit someone. Say, "No hitting," and walk to the other side of the room.

Created by Gary Yorke, PhD, RPT

**7.**

Pretend you are really mad. Take a big breath and blow the anger out S-L-O-W-L-Y.

**8.**

Name one thing you don't like to be told to do. Ask another person to tell you to do that thing, and pretend you are doing it.

**9.**

Say, "I can wait my turn." When do you have to wait your turn?

**10.**

Pretend someone pushed you. Say, "Stop." What would you tell an adult if they asked, "What is going on?"

**11.**

Pretend you are in the bathroom. Now say all your "potty" words, or words you're not allowed to say.

**12.**

Say why children don't like having their toys grabbed.

**13.**

Some adults say to hit something soft when you're mad. What is something soft that you can hit?

**14.**

What is something that is hard to do? Ask another player for help doing that thing.

**15.**

Think of something mean to say and tell another player. Ask the player to say those words and then pretend you are ignoring them.

**16.**

Pretend you just turned over the gingerbread man card and you have to go all the way back to the beginning. Pretend you're going to lose the game now. Show a good way to handle this.

Created by Gary Yorke, PhD, RPT

# ROCK BUDDIES

Children and teens who struggle with appropriate social skills also struggle significantly in the ability to make and maintain friendships with their peers. Many young people, especially those who are more prone to social rejection and isolation, do not really understand what a friend or a healthy friendship looks or feels like emotionally. In this expressive arts intervention, as the child is creating a Rock Buddy, he/she can begin discussing and increasing understanding of how to make and keep friends, what a true friend is, and how to use positive social skills with others.

## SUPPLIES NEEDED:

Assortment of different shapes and sizes of rocks
Glue
Googly eyes
Different colors of paint
Paintbrush for each child
"What is a FRIEND?" handout (pg. 149)

## DIRECTIONS:

1. Instruct each child to pick out a few different rocks they like. They can take time exploring how the texture of each rock feels, what colors they can see in the rocks, and what size rock fits best in their hand.

2. Allow each child to choose what colors of paint they would like to use to paint their rocks. Give each child a paintbrush and instruct them to paint the entire rock. This is a good time to remind the children how to share and take turns.

3. When they are done painting, place the painted rocks on a table and allow to dry.

4. Instruct the children to sit in a circle. As the rocks are drying, you can use the time to explore and process the topic of what makes a good friend.

5. Provide education to the group about what a friend is. It may be helpful to begin the conversation by educating the group that a friend is someone who is nice, is trustworthy, helps them to feel better about themselves, and encourages them to make good decisions.

   Questions to ask include:
   - What is a friend?
   - What makes a good friend?
   - What are three qualities of a friend?
   - How do you know if someone is a friend?
   - What can you do to become a good friend to others?
   - Do you have a good friend?

6. Once the rocks are dry, each child can create his/her Rock Buddy. Each child decides if this will be a person, animal, or creature. They can glue on eyes or otherwise decorate the rock to help them remember how to be a good friend (as well as what a friend is).

7. Each child can take their Rock Buddy home with them, along with the handout "What is a FRIEND?"

# WHAT IS A **FRIEND?**

**F** = Friendly

**R** = Respectful

**I** = Includes me and others

**E** = Enjoyable

**N** = Nice

**D** = Dependable

# WALK THIS WAY

It seems that our world has embraced the symbolism and metaphor of shoes. Shoes often express the personality of the wearer and can seemingly transform us into being beautiful, heroic, sexy, or confident people. Most importantly shoes are memory-laden. Our shoes have walked where we have walked. They carry the memory of our life journey in their very fabric. It has been said that shoes carry our very "souls" in them. Shoes "witness" our walk of life.

This expressive art "shoe" intervention can be used in groups, families, or individual therapy. It is a wonderful way for each person to experience each other from a different perspective by "walking in their shoes." Empathy can be enhanced, as well as an honoring of the path that each member has walked. Creative arts, writing, movement, music, and imagery are used in this intervention.

## SUPPLIES NEEDED:

1 pair of old shoes per person

Hot glue gun and glue sticks

Variety of expressive arts materials including fabric scraps, pipe cleaners, googly eyes, construction paper, magazines, etc.

Scissors

MP3 device or similar music player and audio speakers

## DIRECTIONS FOR GROUP INTERVENTION:

1.  Begin by asking each participant to bring an old pair of shoes that can be used in art. If this would be a financial struggle for group participants, you may want to provide a selection of old shoes for this intervention.

2.  Begin the group by asking everyone to put on the shoes that they brought. Facilitate a group discussion about the symbolism and metaphor of shoes. You may say something such as, *"Our culture has an interesting relationship with shoes. We have imbued them with magical powers that can transport us where our heart desires or give us the powers of our athletic heroes. We speak of shoes in a myriad of ways. "It's as comforting as an old shoe," "step into their shoes for a minute," "wouldn't want to be in their shoes," "waiting for the other shoe to drop," "walk a mile in their shoes," "if the shoe fits wear it," or you're going to "step into their shoes." We have the "shoe" bomber, fairytales of shoes such as Cinderella, Puss 'N Boots, The Wizard of Oz, The Old Woman Who Lived in a Shoe, or "The Red Shoes." We have songs about shoes (I found at least 50 songs about shoes) such as "Blue Suede Shoes," "Boogie Shoes," "These Boots Are Made for Walking," and "Those Shoes." We have just as many movies about shoes as we do songs: "Like Mike," "Kinky Boots," "Get Smart," "Back to the Future" and "Footloose," to name just a few."*

3.  After discussing "shoes" it is time to move. Play a song about shoes and invite everyone to dance to the music as a group. I like to play "Footloose."

4. Next, instruct the group to sit in a comfortable position, take a few deep breaths, and close their eyes; lead them in an imagery exercise. Ask them questions such as:

   - What is your first memory of shoes?

   - What experiences have you had with shoes?

   - What paths have your shoes walked?

   - What experiences have your shoes witnessed?

   - If your shoes could speak, what would they say about their sole (soul)?

   - What experiences have your shoes "stepped into?"

   - Have your shoes danced?

   - What fun have your shoes experienced?

   - What road will your shoes walk on in the future?

   (I find it important in expressive arts to stay in the metaphor. By keeping with the metaphor, it allows a psychological distance, which can often open to more creativity and spontaneity. Talking about shoes and the journey of shoes is much easier and less vulnerable than talking about your own personal journey.)

5. After the imagery is completed, invite everyone to "alter" their shoes. Using available art materials, each person is asked to "alter" their shoes to show the experiences the shoes have been through. Allow plenty of time for this part of the intervention. It is best to have a wide variety of art materials available to enhance the creative experience.

6. When the expressive arts intervention with the shoes has been completed, ask each participant to use their phones or the Internet to find a song or songs that in some way goes with their shoes. Have each person look at their altered shoes while listening to the music chosen using head phones.

7. When they have finished listening to the song(s), ask each person to write a poem about their shoes.

8. Instruct the group members to get into pairs and share their altered shoes, music, and poem with a partner. Allow plenty of time for the sharing.

9. When the group has completed their sharing, bring the group members together and ask everyone to walk around and share their shoes with the group. While the group is sharing, play another song about shoes. I use "Boogie Shoes" and ask participants to "move" with the music while sharing.

10. End the intervention by having the group put all the shoes together in some type of an image that they agree on. It can be any shape or form (such as in the shape of a heart). Take a picture of the shoes and the group to honor and remember their experience together.

This intervention is very powerful and care must be taken to support each person and to allow enough time to create and share.

I hope you enjoy using this as I have. I can't look at my shoes the same way since I created this expressive arts intervention. Now, when I put my tennis shoes on, I swear I can feel their magic and I suddenly I see myself dunking the basketball Michael Jordan style.

Created by John Burr, LCSW, RPT-S

# Chapter 11 — Play Therapy Interventions for Trauma/PTSD

> *The body heals with play,*
> *The mind heals with laughter,*
> *And the spirit heals with JOY.*
>
> —Proverb

According to the Center for Disease Control and Prevention, American children are exposed to all types of complex trauma; the statistics are alarming. The CDC states that one in five Americans is molested as a child, one in four children is beaten by a parent to the point of leaving marks and bruises, one in three couples engage in physical violence, one in four children has an alcoholic parent, and one in eight children witnesses their mother being beaten or hit (van der Kolk, 2015). Trauma can also be experienced in the form of natural or human-caused disasters, such as floods, tornados, and hurricanes; violent crimes, such as kidnapping, rape, murder, or suicide of parents; car crashes, unexpected death or illness, divorce, parental deployment, abandonment, neglect, losing a pet, emotional abuse, war, and community violence, along with a host of other situations that render the child or adult feeling completely helpless and emotionally overwhelmed.

Trauma can be conceptualized as a sudden, overwhelming intense blow or series of blows that assaults the person from the outside (Terr, 1992). This event comes unexpectedly and without warning, leaving the victim utterly helpless, experiencing a debilitating sense of loss of control. The individual's coping strategies are completely overwhelmed, resulting in failure of the primal defense mechanism of a fight/flight response. van der Kolk's 2006 study of trauma has determined that the lack of a successful fight or flight response leaves the child or individual in a frozen state, feeling immobilized or frozen. If the child then dissociates during the traumatic experiences, van der Kolk's research implies that this is the best predictor of a later onset of Posttraumatic Stress Disorder.

## Trauma Symptoms

| | |
|---|---|
| Flashbacks | Nightmares |
| Bedwetting | Sexual reactivity |
| Enuresis and/or encopresis | Extreme clinginess: refusal to be alone |
| Intrusive thoughts | Significant behavior changes |
| Panic attacks | Safety concerns, preoccupation with danger |
| Aggressiveness, angry outbursts | School refusal and avoidance |

In the DSM-5®, there have been several changes to the Posttraumatic Stress Disorder (PTSD) diagnosis. The most overt change was to move PTSD to its own chapter in Stress and Trauma or Related Disorders (instead of including it within the Anxiety Disorders). Changes also include a pediatric onset, with the focus being more on observable changes in behaviors rather than a cognitive description of the event as past Diagnostic and Statistical Manuals have required (American Psychiatric Association, 2014). DSM-5® diagnostic criteria focuses on four diagnostic clusters, including re-experiencing, avoidance, negative cognitions and mood, and arousal.

In children, active re-experiencing typically is manifested in their play. Many children will engage in posttraumatic play, repeating the scene of trauma over and over with their toys, by drawing pictures, or telling the story without filters to anybody and everybody. An example of this could be a young child stating to the grocery clerk, the mailman, the stranger walking down the street, a child on the playground, etc., "My mom was shot with a gun and there was lots and lots of blood and the blood was everywhere." During play or this verbal exchange, the child's affect often will become flat; the eyes appear glazed over. They may seem to lose track of time and place and appear to be in an active state of re-experiencing. If the child's play increases (rather than decreases) anxiety, is ritualized and repetitive, or is difficult to stop and distract, this is a good indicator that the child is engaging in posttraumatic play.

Avoidance is a defense mechanism that many humans employ to protect themselves from the horror of the trauma they have experienced. Children use avoidance as well, but the manifestation of avoidance may be different than in adults. A child may refuse to play altogether following a traumatic event or become highly dysregulated during play. The child may avoid talking about the person or people involved, refuse to go to school or activities, refuse to leave a caregiver's presence, and rage and tantrum if separated even briefly.

Changes in cognition or mood may be demonstrated by a child taking responsibility for the trauma. For example, a child may state, "It is my fault he touched my privates. He told me it was my fault." A child may believe he/she somehow caused the trauma. For example, a child might say, "I was mad at my Dad and told him I hated him. Then the car came and crashed into us and he got hurt and died." Estrangement and withdrawal from others or from previously enjoyed activities may be additional signs of changes in mood and cognition (American Psychiatric Association, 2014).

Arousal in children and teens may appear similar to an adult's response; however, there are developmental differences. Dysregulation, hyper-vigilance, a marked increase in anxiety, fear, nightmares, hyperactivity, impulsivity, and risk-taking, as well as sleep disturbances, are all indicators of arousal (the DSM-5® addresses both the fight and flight aspects associated with the PTSD diagnostic criteria, which is a change from the previous DSM-4®).

## TRAUMA'S IMPACT ON THE BRAIN AND DEVELOPMENT

It is important to understand trauma's impact on the brain, as this causes significant changes to behavior and mood. Without understanding what is happening inside the brain, it is easy for clinicians to misdiagnose the trauma, as the behavioral symptoms of trauma in young children and teens mimic many other mental health disorders, including ADHD, anxiety, CD, and ODD. As discussed in previous chapters, it is imperative that the clinician assess for trauma when treating these disorders, as it is often at the root of undesirable changes in behaviors.

When a trauma occurs, the right brain is "flooded," while the left brain, otherwise known as the anterior cingulate cortex, which is the part of brain that moderates the limbic system, is constricted, and effectively shuts down. Daniel Siegel refers to this as "flipping your lid" as the limbic system hijacks the thinking part of your brain (Siegel & Bryson, 2012). Decreased activity in Broca's area, which is the part of the brain that helps with semantic processing and articulation of speech, results in a decreased ability to communicate thoughts and feelings. Many victims of trauma report feeling "speechless terror" during the event or while processing the event in therapy. An example of this would be a client reporting, "I was screaming for help! I was screaming 'stop!' I was screaming as loud as I could but no sound could come out of my mouth." Researchers believe that this may be caused by decreased activity in this area of the brain (Solomon & Heide, 2005; van der Kolk, 2006; van der Kolk, 2015).

This same reaction in our brains occurs when we are exposed to traumatic reminders or triggers of the event. Since 1999, researchers have been able to effectively look at the brain using technology when it is exposed to traumatic reminders. Bessel van der Kolk was one of the first trauma researchers to utilize PET scans to observe the impact of trauma on a living person's brain. This research has led to changes in the way in which we understand and treat trauma, as well as our developing knowledge about the impact trauma has on not just developing brains, but adult brains as well.

As this "limbic system hijacking" occurs, the areas of the brain that deal with the ability to plan ahead, foresee the consequences of their actions, and prevent themselves from responding inappropriately are less active when under stress. Many children (and adults!) act out in reactivity or impulsivity when this takes place. Traumatic experiences can overwhelm the brain's capacity to process information, which can impact brain structure and can affect memory, learning, the ability to regulate affect, social development, and even moral development (De Bellis et al., 1999). This is important to note, as a child's ability to navigate and understand the world around them is impacted. Too often, children who are experiencing the unending consequences of trauma are met with punitive measures, social isolation, rejection, and unintended further exposure to trauma in the school and social settings, as well as the home environment. Many children who are experiencing a traumatic response in school are labeled as disruptive, defiant, and emotionally unstable, and are either sent to a remote part of the classroom or sent away altogether, further isolating them from their peers and preventing the child from experiencing a "normal" childhood rite of passage.

Episodic memory of the traumatic experience may be stored in the right limbic system indefinitely until the event has been processed fully. This can produce re-experiencing of the images of the traumatic experience, terrifying thoughts, feelings, body sensations, sounds, and smells. It is common during a flashback to lose orientation of time and place and to experience the trauma as if it is happening all over again, including smelling the same smells; hearing the same sounds; experiencing body sensations of touch, constriction, or a racing heart; and feeling the same emotions as the child did in the moment of the actual trauma.

Neuropsychology and neuroimaging research demonstrate that victims of trauma struggle with:

- Concentration/focus
- Paying attention
- Memory
- Being fully engaged in the present

Does this sound familiar as diagnostic criteria for another common childhood diagnosis? Traumatized individuals oftentimes face overwhelming emotions and can't figure out how they feel – physically or emotionally, nor what they need. van der Kolk refers to this as *Alexithymia*, which is the inability to identify the meaning of physical sensations and muscle activation (2015).

An example of how Alexithymia presents could be viewed in the case of how many individuals in acute stages of grief or loss will experience a lack of appetite, sometimes not eating for several days. The individual does not recognize the body's cues for hunger due to the disconnection in the brain's processing of information. When this occurs, the individual is unable to take care of themselves or others. Because they can't internally regulate their emotions, they often become irritated by small incidents and may lash out at others or explode with anger at seemingly small, trivial events.

## EFFECTS OF TRAUMA ON CHILDREN

One of the more devastating effects of trauma on children is that their world belief changes. Children begin to believe that the world is not safe, and my parents *can't* or *chose not to* protect me. This significantly impacts the parent-child relationship and creates a tremendous strain in their attachment pattern. If the parent can't protect the child, then the entire family system is helpless. However, for the child who believes that the parent *chose* not to protect him/her, this creates an entirely different feeling of helplessness and despair.

Children often develop unhealthy coping strategies to defend against vulnerability, referred to as *survival skills.* This helps the child protect against the fear of the unknown which, following a traumatic event, is significantly heightened. Many try to exert control onto their environment, relationships, and self in order to protect against the unknown. It is crucial that the clinician does not prematurely attempt to "take away" or restrict the child's access to their survival skills, but instead, through time, works to augment the survival skills with *living skills*, which are healthy, adaptive coping strategies the child can use throughout life.

> Trauma Is Trauma
> Grief Is Grief
> Loss Is Loss

## HEALING FROM TRAUMA

Each child is different in what he/she needs from the therapeutic process, and it is important to not take a cookie-cutter approach to trauma treatment. That being said, there are some important steps to follow:

- Creating a safe place
- Helping establish trust in the therapeutic relationship
- Assessing and augmenting healthy/positive coping skills
- Telling my story
- Maximizing parent-child trust/attachment
- Understanding who I am now – understanding the posttraumatic self

### Creating a Safe Place and Trust in the Therapeutic Relationship

It can take several play therapy sessions for children who have experienced trauma to learn that the playroom is safe. It should be noted that for some children, the concept of "safe" or "safety" is novel, as they have never experienced safety in their interactions and relationships with their caregivers or adults in their lives. Their reality is that adults will hurt them and there is no such thing as "safety." For these, and all children, giving the child choices from the beginning to instill a healthy sense of control is very important.

Three "Rules"
For Therapists
to Create a
Safe Space

1. Do not walk behind the child and close the door behind you. A better way to initiate therapy is to either walk in front of the child and enter the room first or walk next to him/her and enter together.

2. Allow the child to choose if he/she would like the playroom door open OR closed.

3. Offer the child a choice if he/she would like to come into the first therapy session alone or with the parent/caregiver.

One of the ways you can begin creating a safe place in the playroom, as well as in the therapeutic relationship, is how you approach the child client from the very first moment you say "hello" and introduce yourself. In my practice, I give the child a choice before we even walk into the playroom. I offer permission for the child to either come in independently of their parent/caregiver, or the child can invite them to come with us. For many children, the relief that washes over their face is visibly apparent, and they learn they don't have to be afraid of me or leave their safe person in the waiting room. I imagine being a young child who has experienced significant trauma, and the last thing I would want to do is go alone into a strange place with a strange woman who will then shut the door, leaving me helpless to what she has in store for me in this strange building.

When inviting the child to the playroom, make sure you are aware of your body presence and body language. Be sure that you do not follow your client into the room and shut the door behind them. This can be a very triggering event and will do the opposite of creating safety for the child. Another way to invite him/her in is to either walk in front of the child and welcome him/her to the room, or to walk side by side into the playroom together.

The next step in creating safety is allowing the child another choice: Would he/she like the playroom door open or closed? Some clinicians have balked at this suggestion, as they fear compromising client confidentiality if the door is open. However, I would suggest that it is more important for the child to have a healthy sense of control and decrease in their fear from the beginning than to worry whether others may witness their play therapy session. Remember, much of the trauma children experience happens behind closed doors at the hands of those who are supposed to protect them. Still, it may be prudent for you to discuss this with the child and caregiver and ascertain their comfort level and understanding.

The third step in creating safety is to discuss confidentiality and the limits of confidentiality in the very first session using words a child can comprehend. This helps the child to know what to expect from you as the clinician and to decrease their anxiety about *"what happens if I tell?"* as well as offers security to the child that there is permission for them to talk about hard things, and that as a play therapist, you will help them to be safe physically, mentally, sexually, and emotionally. Engaging in child-centered play therapy for the first several sessions also allows the child to feel in control and gives him/her permission to temper the speed of the play therapy, allowing space and time for the child to explore and express him/herself completely (Landreth, 2002). Remember the important words of caution Landreth expresses, "When we focus on the problem, we lose sight of the child" (2002, p. 85).

## Assessing and Augmenting the Trauma Belief

As we assess the survival skills of the client, it is important that the therapist is in constant communication with the parent and/or caregiver to provide psychoeducation about what the child's survival skills are and how they may manifest behaviorally. This is also an opportunity to address parenting concerns, as well as provide support to a non-offending parent. A child's trauma belief ("it's all my fault," "all boys will hurt me," or "I can never be safe") permeates their conscious as well as unconscious thoughts. They may act out behaviorally to protect themselves from further emotional pain.

As the therapeutic relationship progresses, the play therapist can help the child identify his/her survival skills and learn more adaptive coping strategies to use when triggered or overwhelmed. This process happens gradually as the child learns to trust the therapist. It is important for the therapist to normalize and validate the trauma belief(s), offering supportive statements such as "I can understand why you would feel this way" or "that makes sense to me." It is only when the child feels accepted and validated by the clinician that he/she can trust enough to allow for change and healing to begin. At this stage, the therapist works with the child on reframing the trauma belief. An example of this may be a child initially believing "all boys will hurt me." The therapist gently helps the child to reframe this belief into "Josh hurt me and that doesn't mean that all boys will hurt me."

## Telling My Story

Children NEED to tell *THEIR* story; however, this is not necessarily "the" trauma story that was the initial presenting referral issue. An example of "the" story could be a young girl being referred to therapy following allegations of sexual abuse. This is what "the trauma" is from an adult's perspective. However, once the child has permission to tell her story, the trauma might be something much different. Imagine this same child, in telling her own story, disclosing, "I told my mom that Danny was touching my privates and she didn't believe me. She told me I am a liar." Notice now how this trauma story has changed – could it be that being disbelieved and invalidated by the very person she was expecting comfort from could be more traumatic to this young child than the actual act of abuse and perpetration? The answer is that it depends on the child. This is *their* story, which is one to be honored and validated by their therapist.

A child's story must be told on his/her own timeframe, not the therapist's or parents'. This can sometimes be a difficult process, allowing permission for the child to take their time, due to legal or criminal proceedings and the parents' (and therapist's) anxiety. In my clinical experience, I have noticed that children will often open up about abuse or trauma in a series of disclosures over time. This can be a painful experience for the parent in particular, as the trauma will resurface as the healing process occurs and the child finds the words to tell the story, which can lead to new information regarding the traumatic events. Now remember, a child can tell his/her story without ever saying a verbal word – this is the power of play therapy. A child will tell the story in the language that makes most sense to the child.

Creating a trauma narrative gives empowerment and a voice to one who has felt voiceless and helpless. Children learn mastery over their fear and feelings of helplessness as they begin to make sense of the events that have happened around them and to them. For the clients whom I've worked with, this has not always been a chronological timeline of events. For some children, the narrative revolves around the intensity of the emotions involved, the level of fear felt, and the repairing of trust in the adults and caretakers, while others *do* need a timeline of events that have occurred to give a concrete story to their young mind.

### Maximizing the Parent-Child Relationship

It is crucial to have ongoing engagement with the non-offending parent(s) or permanent caregivers throughout the therapeutic process. As the child is working through the trauma, the trust between parent and child also needs repair work and strengthening. Remember, one of the effects of trauma is the belief that the world is not safe and the parents can't protect the child (this is true regardless of the nature of the traumatic experience). A child needs to feel safe in order to heal and engage in the world in a healthy, adaptive manner, and a renewed relationship with the parent is necessary for this to occur.

A child can only progress as far as the parent is willing to progress, as the child is the most vulnerable and least powerful member of the family system. The parent is the individual with the power to create safety in the home and in their relationship. As the therapeutic process continues, engaging the parent in play therapy with the child is an important and often overlooked part of the healing process.

### Integrating the Pre- and Post-Trauma Self

This last phase of the healing process is a crucial component in allowing for the trauma to become an integrated part of the child's *Self*, without it becoming the sole identity. Many clients lament, "I just want to go back to how it used to be" or "I just want to be the old me again." Feeling a sense of loss for the "old" parts of self is a normal and common part of the grieving process that many individuals who have undergone a traumatic event experience. There is a loss of innocence, loss of relationships, and loss of self that occurs – especially if the trauma had been a recurrent experience.

Utilizing the Dialectical Behavior Therapy (DBT) concept of radical acceptance is an important part of the integration of pre- and post-trauma selves. Dietz writes, "Radical means complete and total. It's when you accept something from the depths of your soul. When you accept it in your mind, in your heart, and even with your body. It's total and complete. When you've radically accepted something, you're not fighting it. It's when you stop fighting reality. That's what radical acceptance is" (Dietz, n.d.). Clients young and old must be able to accept that the traumatic experience did in fact happen, that there is nothing they can do to change the fact that this event happened, *and* that it does not have to define who they are as a person, as their *Self*, or how they navigate the world moving forward. By accepting that these events did in fact happen and allowing this to be only a chapter of their life story, true healing and integration can occur. Moving forward can and does happen! And most importantly, the client resolves to write the rest of their story.

## PLAY THERAPY AND TRAUMA

Play gives words to the unspeakable. For most of us, there are not adequate words to describe the terror and helplessness one feels during that moment of trauma. Play therapy can help give language to the child's story as well as bring the terror, fear, and loss to a tangible, physical state of being (rather than swimming around internally in an intangible experience of constant re-experiencing). As we have discussed extensively in previous chapters, play therapy can take on many forms. For children who've experienced trauma, I propose utilizing an integrated prescriptive approach to play therapy, meaning that there is blending of different theoretical orientations in the application of treatment (Gil, 1991). At times, utilizing a child-centered approach is best practice; however, through the course of treatment, a more directive or Trauma-Focused Cognitive Behavioral Therapy (TF-CBT) approach is needed. What is most important is for the clinician to become a trauma-informed therapist and seek out additional training in trauma and play therapy to ensure that he/she is adequately trained to help the child and parents in their healing journey.

# CREATING MY SAFE PLACE SAND TRAY

An 11-year-old client's safe place sand tray

In the early stages of trauma-based play therapy, helping your client to understand and define for themselves the concept of "safety" and feeling "safe" is very helpful in developing a strong therapeutic relationship between the child and therapist. Utilizing a sand tray and symbolic metaphor can be useful, especially when there are no words or verbal language to articulate how the child has experienced the opposite feeling of safety during the traumatic experience. In this directive sand tray intervention, the therapist first engages the child in conversation about what the word "safety" means and then asks the child to create in the sand tray his/her own version of a safe place. This may be a real place, a fantasy place, a place the child wants to go to, or a place he/she has visited. There is no instruction nor any specifics given, as the child gets to be the director and visionary in this process.

After the child reports that the sand tray is complete, you may want to process with the child what the sand tray means to him/her and what each figurine means, as well as how the child feels when looking at the sand tray. Be mindful that as the therapist, you do not try to rescue the child in the sand tray or put your own representations of safety in the sand. In this intervention, especially in the early stages of treatment, the child may have a more chaotic representation or themes of lurking danger in his/her sand tray. This is part of the healing process and will give you a lot of information about where the child currently is in the trauma healing process.

One of the ways I will document with the child their progress in treatment is to allow the child to take a picture of the sand trays throughout the therapeutic journey. As a termination activity, we

160

will create "A Safe Place" sand tray and compare the initial safe place to the safe place he/she can take home as the therapy services are ending. There is usually a stark contrast in the child's sand trays from the beginning of therapy compared with the end of therapy, as his/her understanding of safety has evolved and become an integrated part of the child's understanding and concept of self.

## SUPPLIES NEEDED:

> Sand tray
> Variety of figurines

## DIRECTIONS:

**1.** Instruct the client to create a sand tray that represents their safe place. Allow as much time as needed for this to be completed.

**2.** Ask the child to tell you a story about his/her safe place, being mindful to *not* ask questions like "why did you do...?"

**3.** Ask the child, "What does 'safe' mean to you?" You may want to explore how a child can experience feeling safe emotionally and physically, as well as help some children who have never experienced a sense of safety understand the meaning of this word.

# MY SECRET BOX

Many children who have experienced trauma, abuse, and/or neglect often have many secrets, whether they have been groomed by the perpetrator to keep quiet or fear telling others what has happened to them, for fear of rejection, retaliation, or indifference on behalf of the adults around them (Gil, 1991). Children will often disclose abuse or neglect in layers and through a series of disclosures as they gain trust in the therapeutic relationship and with the clinician. For some therapists, this can be a frustrating experience, especially if he/she is expecting a verbal disclosure all at once.

Due to the nature of sexual abuse, where it is much more likely that the client will have had a direct relationship with the perpetrator, either as a family member or close friend, he/she may not be ready to disclose the abuse for fear that the loved one will be hurt or punished in some way. Many abused children feel a sense of responsibility to their abusers and for the abuse occurring to them.

Teaching children who have experienced abuse and/or neglect the concept of trust and safety takes time. This intervention can be a gateway between therapist and client, to begin testing the trust as it is secured over time. By giving your client the opportunity to let go of secrets, the child feels permission to be free from the burdens he/she has been carrying. The client chooses the pacing of this activity, as it is imperative that the child feel a sense of control over any disclosure of abuse or secret-keeping (by keeping the secret, the child has experienced some level of control in a situation that has otherwise been completely outside the realm of his/her control).

## SUPPLIES NEEDED:

> Any size box with a lid
> Markers
> Pencils

## DIRECTIONS:

1. Instruct the child to decorate the outside of the box however they would like to, understanding that this is their secret box.

2. Process with your client the definition of what a secret is and what emotions the client feels inside when keeping a secret.

3. Ask the child to write down or draw a picture of any secrets they are currently keeping, reminding them that they do not have to tell you or show you now, unless they choose to.

4. Once the child has finished the writings or drawings, they can fold up their secrets and put them into their secret box. The child can then secure the box closed if they choose to do so and choose a safe place for the therapist to keep the box until the next session.

5. At the next session, ask the child to choose one secret out of the box that they feel ready to show to you. Explore what this secret is, what it means to the child, and the fears or anxiety associated with it.

# TELLING MY STORY WITH MY BLANCO DOLL

*11-year-old's Blanco doll story*

A child's trauma story does not have to be verbal, as often there are no words to adequately describe how the emotions felt or what the child was/is thinking (remember Alexthymia). However, by creating an art-based expressive "story," the child can begin creating a narrative of the experience. Using a My Blanco Doll is an excellent resource, as it gives the child a blank slate as well as a container for big feelings and emotions. By creating a narrative of the trauma, the child can begin to form needed language as well as feel empowered. Dr. Mary Ann Peabody once said, "We can't change the child's story, but what we can change is how the child feels about themselves in their story" (Association for Play Therapy, 2011).

## SUPPLIES NEEDED:

My Blanco doll                Stickers, tape, etc.
Washable markers          Blank paper

## DIRECTIONS:

**1.** Provide a clean My Blanco doll and washable markers for the child.

**2.** Instruct the child to draw how he/she is feeling or to draw the story onto the toy product.

**3.** Allow for as much time as needed, instructing the child that the drawing doesn't need to be perfect and that he/she can be the boss of what it looks like.

**4.** Once the child feels that the story is ready, ask about it. Remember, it does not need to be "the" trauma story!

**5.** Explore the child's thoughts and feelings, both about what immediate feelings come up, and as how it feels to talk about the story. You may want to ask questions such as, "I wonder how the monkey feels right now as we are talking about its story" or "Wow, I wonder what that must have felt like to the monkey?"

**6.** At the end of the session, you may want to take a picture of the story. If the child would like a copy of the picture, you can provide that.

# BOUNDIN'

Boundin' is an intervention for all clients who have experienced difficult life experiences, ranging from normal life transitions, to smaller pains, such as hurt feelings and disappointments, to the big traumas of life. This intervention can be used in the beginning, middle, or end of treatment. Boundin' is effective in teaching the concept of resiliency and helps to validate the client's story and triumph in finding a voice again. This intervention can be used in individual, family or group therapy. If used in family or group, the therapist can help increase skills in reflective listening and help members to process one another's reactions to build empathy and understanding.

## SUPPLIES NEEDED:

> Pixar's Boundin'® video
> Puppets
> Optional: Bouncy balls, Magic scratch paper, lyrics to Boundin'

## DIRECTIONS:

1. Instruct group members to sit in a circle. If working one-on-one, ask your client to sit in a comfortable position.
2. Provide psychoeducation about the ups and downs of life. This means that life does not always work according to our plans and sometimes unexpected hurts may happen, as well as disappointments and times of struggle. Explain that resilience is the ability to go through these difficult things and figure out how to get back up.
3. Watch the video "Boundin.'"
4. Ask your client to identify events or things that have been difficult. Process how the client relates to the video.
5. Instruct the client to create and perform a puppet show demonstrating the difficult event and how he/she can get back up.

## ADDITIONAL PLAY THERAPY ACTIVITIES:

### CBT METHOD:

Explain the difference between negative/destructive thoughts and positive/realistic thoughts. Describe how our thoughts influence feelings and behavior about the events that happen.

Read the lyrics to the movie Boundin' and emphasize key points. Have the client identify a positive statement in the lyrics and write it on the magic scratch paper.

### EXPERIENTIAL:

Buy or make bouncy balls. Have the client throw the ball at the ground and state something that was difficult or painful to go through; then, when the ball comes back up, the client can tell how he/she recovered from it. The bouncy ball can be taken home as a reminder of what was learned in the session.

Created by Holly Willard, LCSW

# THE WALLED-OFF HEART INTERVENTION

The Walled-Off Heart intervention is for any client who has experienced attachment issues or attachment wounds in relationships. It is applicable for the full spectrum of attachment issues, including trauma, rejection, abandonment, foster care, failed adoption, neglect, abuse, death, and Reactive Attachment Disorder.

The intervention is most appropriate for use in the middle phase of treatment. It requires therapeutic rapport and understanding of attachment history because you are processing triggering events and deep feelings. The therapist can describe attachment using the metaphors early in treatment, but it is not recommended to start labeling events or processing until therapeutic trust is established and healthy coping skills are being utilized.

The intervention can take several sessions to process and complete depending on the client's level of trauma and willingness to discuss issues. The intervention can also assist in creating a timeline and narrative of the trauma.

**SUPPLIES NEEDED:**

Paper and markers
Sand tray, cookie cutter hearts or fences

**DIRECTIONS:**

**1.** Explain trauma and attachment. You may say something along the lines of, *"When you are a baby, if your needs are met, then you learn the world is safe and you can trust adults to take care of you, and your heart is open to others. If not, you learn that the world is unsafe and you can't count on others. Or maybe, something bad happened that made you feel unsafe (trauma), so you start to build walls around your heart to protect yourself."*

**2.** Instruct your client to identify events or things that happened that built walls around his/her heart. If using paper, instruct him/her to draw and label the walls. Or if using a sand tray, have the client build the walls with the cookie cutters or fences.

**3.** Next, identify people in the client's life and how close they are to the client's heart (if using a sand tray, have figures available to represent the people). Discuss how the child could allow the safe people closer to his/her heart (you can use ladders over the walls).

**4.** Explain that at some point in life, we all need walls to protect us and that walls aren't always bad. But now the child can decide who is safe and can choose to let them in.

**Additional ideas:** Take a picture so in future sessions you can reference it or rebuild the heart the client has created. Example: If the child pushed the caregiver away, after a really good day in session, the picture can help to normalize the fear of getting closer because of the hurt previously experienced.

Created by Holly Willard, LCSW

# References

For your convenience, purchasers can download and print
worksheets and handouts from www.pesi.com/mellenthin

Abramowitz, J. S., & Jacoby, R. J. (2014). Obsessive-Compulsive Disorder in the DSM-5®. *Clinical Psychology Science and Practice, 21*(3), 221–234.

American Academy of Child and Adolescent Psychiatry. (July 2013). Obsessive-Compulsive disorder in children and adolescents. Retrieved from: http://www.aacap.org/AACAP/Families and_Youth/Facts_for_Families/ FFF-Guide/Obsessive-Compulsive-Disorder-In-Children-And-Adolescents-060.aspx

American Psychological Association. (2014). *Diagnostic and Statistical Manual of Mental Disorders* (5th ed.). Washington, DC: Author.

Anderson, M., Cesur, R., & Tekin, E. (2015). Youth depression and future criminal behavior. *Economic Inquiry, 53*(1), 294–317. doi:10.1111/ecin.12145

Association for Play Therapy. (2016). Why play therapy? Retrieved from: http://www.a4pt.org/page/ WhyPlayTherapy

Association for Play Therapy. (Jan 29, 2011). *Play therapy works!* [video file]. Retrieved from: https://www.youtube. com/watch?v=_4ovwAdxCs0

Atkins Loria, S., Macdonald, H., & Mitterling, C. (2015). Young African American men and the diagnosis of conduct disorder: The neo-colonization of suffering. *Clinical Social Work Journal, 43*(4), 431–441. doi:10.1007/s10615-015-0531-8

Autism Society of America. (2017). What Is Autism? [Blog post]. Retrieved from: http://www.autism-society. org/what-is/

Axline, V. M., & Carmichael, L., (1947). *Play Therapy: The Inner Dynamics of Childhood.* Boston: Houghton Mifflin Co.

Baron-Cohen, S. (1995). *Mindblindness: An Essay on Autism and Theory of Mind.* Cambridge, MA: MIT Press/ Bradford Books.

Baron-Cohen, S. (2000). Autism and theory of mind. In J., Hartley, & A. Branthwaite (Eds.), *The Applied Psychologist,* 181–194. New York, NY: Taylor and Francis.

Baggerly, J. (2004). The effects of child-centered group play therapy on self-concept, depression, and anxiety of children who are homeless. *International Journal of Play Therapy, 13*(2), 31–51.

Barkley, R. A. (2000). Commentary on the multimodal treatment study of children with ADHD. *Journal of Abnormal Child Psychology, 28*(6), 595.

Barry, L., & Burlew, S. (2004). Using social stories to teach choice and play skills to children with autism. *Focus on Autism and Other Developmental Disabilities, 19*(1), 45–51.

Bartz, J. A. (2012). Oxytocin, attachment, betrayal, and self-interest: A commentary on "oxytocin modulates the link between adult attachment and cooperation through reduced betrayal aversion" by Carsten K. W. De Dreu, *Psychoneuroendocrinology, 37*(7), 1106. doi:10.1016/j.syneuen.2011.10.033

Beaumont, R., & Sofronoff, K. (2008). A multi-component social skills intervention with children with Asperger Syndrome: The junior detective training program. *The Journal of Child Psychology and Psychiatry, 49*(7), 743–753.

Boer, O. E., & Tranent, P. J. (2013). Conceptualizing the relationship between maternal parenting style and adolescent self-esteem: A pragmatic approach. *Journal of Relationships Research, 4*(7). Retrieved from: http:// dx.doi.org.libproxy2.usc.edu/10.1017/jrr.2013.5

Booth, P. B., & Jernberg, A. M. (2010). *Theraplay.* San Francisco, CA: Jossey-Bass.

Bratton, S. C., Ceballos, P. L., Sheely-Moore, A. L., Proncehnko, Y., & Jones, L. D. (2013). Head start early mental health intervention: Effects of child-centered play therapy on disruptive behaviors. *International Journal of Play Therapy, 22*(1), 28–42.

Bratton, S., Ray, D., Rhine, T., & Jones, L. (2005). The efficacy of play therapy with children: A meta-analytic review of treatment outcomes. *American Psychological Association. Professional Psychology: Research and Practice, 26*(4), 376–390.

Brown, H. M., Meiser-Stedman, R., Woods, H., & Lester, K. J. (2014). Cognitive vulnerabilities for depression and anxiety in childhood: Specificity of anxiety sensitivity and rumination. *Behavioural and Cognitive Psychotherapy, 44*(1), 30–42. doi: 10.1017/S1352465814000472

Buchheim, A., Heinrichs, M., George, C., Pokorny, D., Koops, E., Henningsen, P., & Gündel, H. (2009). Oxytocin enhances the experience of attachment security. *Psychoneuroendocrinology, 34*(9), 1417–1422. doi:10.1016/j.psyneuen.2009.04.002

Christian, K. M., Russ, S., & Short, E. J. (2011). Pretend play processes and anxiety: Considerations for the play therapist. *International Journal of Play Therapy, 20*(4), 179–192. Retrieved from: http://libproxy.usc.edu/login?url=http://search.proquest.com.libproxy1.usc.edu/docview/889441475?accountid=14749

Coplan, J. (2010). *Making Sense of Autistic Spectrum Disorders*. NY: Bantam Books.

Cotugno, A. (2009). Social competence and social skills training and intervention for children with autism spectrum disorders. *Journal of Autism Development Disorder, 39*(0), 1268–1277.

Crenshaw, D. A., & Kenney-Noziska, S. (2014). Therapeutic presence in play therapy. *International Journal of Play Therapy, 23*(1), 31-43. Retrieved from: http://dx.doi.org.libproxy1.usc.edu/10.1037/a0035480

Dawson, G., McPartland, J., & Ozonoff, S. (2002). *A Parent's Guide to Asperger's Syndrome & High-Functioning Autism*. NY: The Guilford Press.

De Bellis, M. D., Clark, D. B., Casey, B. J., Giedd, J. N., Boring, A. M., Frustaci, K., & Ryan, N. D. (1999). Developmental traumatology part II: Brain development. *Society of Biological Psychiatry, 45,* 1271–1284.

DeHart, T., Pelham, B. W., & Tennen, H. (2006). What lies beneath: Parenting style and implicit self-esteem. *Journal of Experimental Social Psychology, 42*(1), 1–17. doi:10.1016/j.jesp.2004.12.005

Diamond, G., & Josephson, A. (2005). Family-based treatment research: A 10-year update. *Journal of the American Academy of Child & Adolescent Psychiatry, 44*(9), 872–887. doi:10.1097/01.chi.0000169010.96783.4e

Dietz, L. (n.d.). Radical Acceptance Part 1.[blog post]. Retrieved from: http://www.dbtselfhelp.com/html/radical_acceptance_part_1.html

Eller, S. M. (2011). Play therapy with adults. *Play Therapy Magazine, 6*(2), 16–20.

Exkorn, K. S. (2005). *The Autism Sourcebook*. NY: HarperCollins Publishers.

Fine, S., & Willingham, E. J. (2011). Play therapy. In J. L. Longe (Ed.), *The Gale Encyclopedia of Children's Health* (2nd ed.), 3, 1756–1759. Detroit: Gale. Retrieved from: http://go.galegroup.com.libproxy1.usc.edu/ps/i.do?id=GALE%7CCCX1918500598&sid=summon&v=2.1&u=usocal_main&it=r&p=GVRL&sw=w&asid=bd2277d52f69ff8be145583647101b20

Fraser (2011). *Developing Appropriate Social Skills in Children with Autism*. Minneapolis, MN: Author.

Frojd, S., Nissinen, E., Pelkonen, M., Marttunen, M., Koivisto, A., & Kaltiala-Heino, R. (2008). Depression and school performance in middle adolescent boys and girls. *Journal of Adolescence, 31*(4), 485–498. doi:10.1016/j.adolescence.2007.08.006

Garza, Y., & Bratton, S. (2005). School-based child-centered play therapy with Hispanic children: Outcomes and cultural considerations. *International Journal of Play Therapy, 14*(1), 51–79.

Gathright, M. M., & Tyler, L. H. (2014). *Disruptive Behaviors in Children and Adolescents*. Little Rock, AK: University of Arkansas for Medical Sciences.

Gledhill, J., & Hodes, M. (2015). Management of depression in children and adolescents: Depression in young people. *Progress in Neurology and Psychiatry, 19*(2), 28–33. doi:10.1002/pnp.375

Gil, E. (1991). *The Healing Power of Play*. New York, NY: The Guilford Press.

Gil, E. (2015). *Play in Family Therapy*. New York, NY: The Guilford Press.

Gil, E., & Terr, L. (2010). *Working with Children to Heal Interpersonal Trauma: The Power of Play*. New York, NY: The Guilford Press.

Gold-Steinberg, S., & Logan, D. (1999). Integrating play therapy in the treatment of children with obsessive-compulsive disorder. *American Journal of Orthopsychiatry, 69*(4), 495–503.

Grant, R. J. (2015). Family play counseling with children affected by autism. In E. J. Green, J. N. Baggerly, & A. C. Myrick (Eds.), *Counseling Families: Play-Based Treatment*. Lanham, MD: Rowman & Littlefield.

Grant, R. J. (2016a). *AutPlay Therapy for Children and Adolescents on the Autism Spectrum: A Behavioral Play-Based Approach*. New York, NY: Routledge.

Grant, R. J. (2016b). *Play-Based Interventions for Autism Spectrum Disorders and Other Developmental Disabilities*. New York, NY: Routledge.

Gresham, F. M., Cook, C. R., Crews, S. D., & Kern, L. (2004). Social skills training for children and youth with emotional and behavioral disorders: Validity considerations and future directions. *Behavioral Disorders, 30*(1), 32–46.

Hannesdottir, D. K., & Ollendick, T. H. (2007). The role of emotion regulation in the treatment of child anxiety disorders. *Clinical Child and Family Psychology Review, 10*(3), 275–293. doi:10.1007/s10567-007-0024-6

Jaycox, L., Stein, B., Paddock, S., Miles, J., Chandra, A., Meredith, L., Tanielian, T., Hickey, S., & Burnam, A. (2009). Impact of teen depression on academic, social, and physical functioning. *Pediatrics, 124*(4), 596–605. doi:10.1542/peds.2008-3348. PMID: 19736259. Retrieved from: http://www.ncbi.nlm.nih.gov/pubmed/19736259

Josefi, O., & Ryan, V. (2004). Non-directive play therapy for young children with autism: A case study. *Clinical Child Psychology and Psychiatry, 9*, 533–551.

Kaduson, H. G. (2006a). Release play therapy for children with posttraumatic stress disorder. In H. G. Kaduson & C. E. Schaefer (Eds.), *Short-Term Play Therapy for Children, 2*, 3–21. New York, NY: The Guilford Press.

Kaduson, H. G. (2006b). Short-term play therapy for children with attention-deficit/hyperactivity disorder. In H. G. Kaduson & C. E. Schaefer (Eds.), *Short-Term Play Therapy for Children, 2*, 101-144. New York, NY: The Guilford Press.

Kaduson, H. G., & Schaefer, C. E. (2006). *Short-Term Play Therapy for Children* (2nd ed.). New York, NY: The Guilford Press.

Kahn, T. R., & Hanna, F. J. (2000). Disruptive behavior disorders in children and adolescents: How do girls differ from boys? *Journal of Counseling and Development. 78*(3), 267–275.

Knell, S. M., & Dasari, M. (2006). Cognitive-behavioral play therapy for children with anxiety and phobias. In H. G. Kaduson & C. E. Schaefer (Eds.), *Short-Term Play Therapy for Children, 2*, 22-50. New York, NY: The Guildford Press.

Kottman, T. (2013). *Play Therapy: Basics and Beyond* (2nd ed.). Alexandria, VA: American Counseling Association.

Kronenberger, W. G., & Meyer, R. G. (2001). *The Child Clinician's Handbook* (2nd ed.). Needham, MA: Allyn and Bacon.

Krysan, M., Moore, K. A., & Zill, N. (2010). Identifying successful families: An overview of constructs and selected measures. *Child Trends, Inc.* U.S. Department of Health and Human Services. Retrieved from: http://www.aspe.hhs.gov

Landreth, G. (2002). *Play Therapy: The Art of the Relationship*. New York, NY: Brunner-Routledge.

Laushey, K., & Heflin, L. J. (2000). Enhancing social skills of kindergarten children with autism through the training of multiple peers as tutors. *Journal of Autism and Developmental Disorders, 30*(3), 183–193.

Lowenstein, L. (2006). *Creative Intervention for Children of Divorce*. Toronto, Canada: Champion Press.

Lowenstein, L. (1999). *Creative Interventions for Troubled Children and Youth*. Toronto, Canada: Champion Press.

Luby, J. L. (2010). Preschool depression: The importance of identification of depression early in development. *Current Directions in Psychological Science, 19*(2), 91.

Lyness, D. (2015). The Story of Self-Esteem [PDF file]. Retrieved from: https://kidshealth.org/en/kids/self-esteem.html.

Meany-Walen, K. K., Bratton, S. C., & Kottman, T. (2014). Effects of Adlerian play therapy on reducing students' disruptive behaviors. *Journal of Counseling & Development, 92*(1), 47–56. doi:10.1002/j.1556-6676.2014.00129.x

Miller, G. E., & Prinz, R. J. (2003). Engagement of families in treatment for childhood conduct problems. *Behavior Therapy, 34*, 517–534.

Monteiro, M. (2016). *Family Therapy and the Autism Spectrum: Autism Conversations in Narrative Practice*. New York, NY: Routledge.

Moor, J. (2008). *Playing, Laughing and Learning with Children on the Autism Spectrum: A Practical Resource of Play Ideas for Parents and Caregivers*. Philadelphia, PA: Jessica Kingsley Publishers.

Mrug, S., Hoza, B., & Gerdes, A. C. (2001). Children with attention-deficit/hyperactivity disorder: Peer relationships and peer-oriented interventions. *New Directions for Child and Adolescent Development, 2001*(91), 51. doi:10.1002/cd.5

Myrick, A. C., & Green, E. J. (2012). Incorporating play therapy into evidence-based treatment with children affected by obsessive-compulsive disorder. *International Journal of Play Therapy, 21*(2), 74–86.

O'Connor, C., & Stagnitti, K. (2011). Play, behavior, language and social skills: The comparison of play and a non-play intervention within a specialist school setting. *Research in Developmental Disabilities, 32*(0), 1205–1211.

Parker, N., & O'Brien, P. (2011). Play therapy: reaching the child with autism. *International Journal of Special Education, 26*(1), 80–87.

Powell, M. L., Newgent, R. A., & Lee, S. M. (2006). Group cinematherapy: Using metaphor to enhance adolescent self-esteem. *The Arts in Psychotherapy, 33*(3), 247-253. doi:10.1016/j.aip.2006.03.004

Porter, M. L., Hernandez-Reif, M., & Jessee, P. (2009). Play therapy: A review. *Early Child Development and Care, 179*(8), 1025–1040. doi:10.1080/03004430701731613

Portrie-Bethke, T. L., Hill, N. R., & Bethke, J. G. (2009). Strength-based mental health counseling for children with ADHD: An integrative model of adventure-based counseling and Adlerian play therapy. *Journal of Mental Health Counseling, 31*(4), 323–339.

Post, P. (1999). Impact of child-centered play therapy on the self-esteem, locus of control, and anxiety of at-risk 4th, 5th, and 6th grade students. *International Journal of Play Therapy, 8*(2), 1–18. Retrieved from: http://libproxy.usc.edu/login?url=http://search.proquest.com.libproxy1.usc.edu/docview/614360231?accountid=14749

Quirmbach, L., Lincoln, A., Feinberg, M., Ingersoll, B., & Andrews, S. (2008). Social stories: Mechanisms of effectiveness in increasing game play skills in children diagnosed with autism spectrum disorder. Using a pretest posttest repeated measures randomized control group design. *Springer Science + Business Media, LLC.* doi:10.1007/s/10803-008-0628-9

Ray, D. C., Lee, K. R., Meany-Walen, K. K., Carlson, S. E., Carnes-Holt, K. L., & Ware, J. N. (2013). Use of toys in child-centered play therapy. *International Journal of Play Therapy, 22*(1), 43–57.

Ray, D. C., Schottelkorb, A., & Tsai, M. (2007). Play therapy with children exhibiting symptoms of attention deficit/hyperactivity disorder. *International Journal of Play Therapy 16*(2), 95–111.

Rezvan, S., Bahrami, F., Abedi, M., MacLeod, C., Doost, H. R. N, & Ghasemi, V. (2012). Attachment insecurity as a predictor of obsessive-compulsive symptoms in female children. *Counseling Psychology Quarterly, 25*(4), 403–415.

Riviere, S. (2009). Short-term play therapy for children with disruptive behavior disorders. In H. G. Kaduson & C. E. Schaefer (Eds.), *Short-Term Play Therapy for Children* (2nd ed.). New York, NY: The Guilford Press.

Rubin, L. (2012). Playing in the autism spectrum. In L. Gallo-Lopez & L. C. Rubin (Eds.), *Play Based Interventions for Children and Adolescents with Autism Spectrum Disorders,* 19–35. NY: Routledge.

Trzesniewski, K., Moffit, T., Poulton, R., Donnellan, B., Robins, R., & Caspi, A. (2006). Low self-esteem during adolescence predicts poor health, criminal behavior, and limited economic prospects during adulthood. *Developmental Psychology, 42*(2), pp. 381-390. Doi: 10.1037/0012-1649.42.2.381

Schaefer, C. E., & O'Connor, K. J. (1983). *Handbook of Play Therapy.* New York, NY: Wiley.

Shoakazemi, M., Javid, M. M., Tazekand, F. E., Rad, Z. S., & Gholami, N. (2012). The effect of group play therapy on reduction of separation anxiety disorder in primitive school children. *Procedia—Social and Behavioral Sciences, 69,* 95–103. doi:10.1016/j.sbspro.2012.11.387

Shore, A. (1999). *Affect Regulation and the Origin of the Self: The Neurobiology of Emotional Development.* Hillsdale, NJ: Erlbaum.

Siegel, D., & Bryson, T. (2012). *The Whole-Brain Child: 12 Revolutionary Strategies to Nurture Your Child's Developing Mind.* New York, NY: Random House Publishing Group.

Solomon, E. P., & Heide, K. M. (2005). The biology of trauma: Implications for treatment. *Journal of Interpersonal Violence, 20,* 51–60.

Siahkalroudi, S. G., & Bahri, M. Z. (2015). Effectiveness of cognitive behavioral play therapy group on self-esteem and social skills in girl's elementary school. *Journal of Scientific Research and Development, 2*(4), 114–120.

Terr, L. (1992). *Too Scared to Cry, Psychic Trauma in Childhood.* New York, NY: Basic Books.

van der Kolk, B. (2006). Clinical implications of neuroscience research in PTSD. *Annals of the New York Academy of Sciences, 1071*(1), 277–293. doi:10.1196/annals.1364.022

van der Kolk, B. (2015). *The Body Keeps the Score.* New York, NY: Penguin Books.

VanFleet, R. (2014). *Filial Therapy: Strengthening Parent-Child Relationships Through Play* (3rd ed.). Sarasota, FL: Professional Resource Press.

Yarbro, J., Mahaffey, B., Abramowitz, J., & Kashdan, T. B. (2013). Recollections of parent-child relationships, attachment insecurity, and obsessive-compulsive beliefs. *Personality and Differences, 54,* 355–360.

Zhou, X., Hetrick, S., Cujipers, P., Qin, B., Barth, J., Whittington, C., Cohen, D., Del Giovane, C., Liu, Y., Michael, K., Zhang, Y., Weisz, J., & Xie, P. (2015). Comparative efficacy and acceptability of psychotherapies for depression in children and adolescents: A systemic review and network meta-analysis. *World Psychiatry, 14*(2), pp. 207-222. doi: 10.1002/wps.20217

Made in the USA
Monee, IL
06 June 2024

59517532R00103